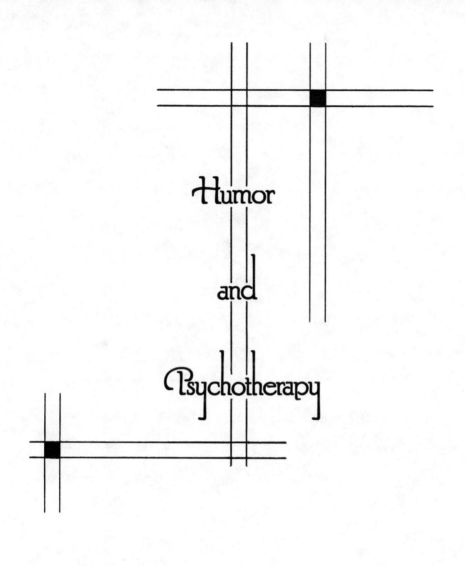

Humor

and

Psychotherapy

Humor and Psychotherapy

THOMAS L. KUHLMAN, Ph.D.
Mendota Mental Health Institute

DORSEY PROFESSIONAL BOOKS

DOW JONES-IRWIN
Homewood, Illinois 60430

ISBN 0-87094-436-3

Library of Congress Catalog Card No. 83–73365

Printed in the United States of America

1 2 3 4 5 6 7 8 9 0 BC 1 0 9 8 7 6 5 4

Acknowledgments

The author wishes to gratefully acknowledge the various and sundry contributions of the following toward the completion of this book: K. C., the coffee and tobacco industries of the United States of America, Roger Cohen, S. F., Mel Gale, Wilma Gilbert, Marshall Ginsburg, Jeff Goldstein, Marge Grinnell and Cathy Pond, Elissa Hamilton, Mark Heintzelman, Michael Kaye, Birsen Khaya, Barbara Killinger, Leo G. Kuhlman, Marion Lindblad-Goldberg, G. L. (with regrets), my loyal subjects of MU, Bob Miller, Harvey Mindess, Larainne Paskey and Jane Morris, Dave Pollock, PES (before The Wake), the inventor of the semicolon, Ron Shanovich, Dawn U. at the U.W. campus McDonalds (three creams—one sugar), Larry Ventis, Cathy Vest, Lou and John at the Washington Host, Susan and Wayne Wooley, and Bob Zechnich.

Finally, my deepest gratitude and love to Barbara Capuano Kuhlman, *sine qua non* to the author and his work. On a related subject, hello to Chris and Natalie, even if it will be 10 years before you are able to read this.

This book was written at the Cincinnati General Hospital cafeteria (carpeted side), the Circle bar of the Washington Host, and the Desperation Room of the University of Wisconsin Memorial Library. It is dedicated to Drs. Quereshi, Bieliauskas, and Weiner. To these men, whom I will never address by their first names, I pose the almost rhetorical question embedded by Big Chuck into the collective unconscious of late-night-TV-watching Clevelanders everywhere: "I turned out alright . . . didn't I?"

Thomas L. Kuhlman

Permission Acknowledgments

The author wishes to express his appreciation to the following for granting permission to reproduce significant portions of case materials that were previously published and copyrighted in other sources.

Psychoanalytic Quarterly
   (Zwirling case p. 29; reference p. 121)

Samiksa—Journal of the Indian Psychoanalytic Society, Calcutta
   (Grotjahn case p. 34; reference p. 115)

American Journal of Psychiatry
   (Poland case p. 36; reference p. 118)
   (Kubie case p. 87; reference p. 116)

Dr. Barbara Killinger
   (case p. 39; reference p. 116)

Noyes Press
   (Kadis & Winick case p. 40; reference p. 116)

Alfred A. Knopf Inc.
   (Frankl case p. 49; reference p. 114)

Dr. Ronald E. Smith & *Behavior Therapy*
   (case p. 47; reference p. 119)

Behavioral Neuropsychiatry
   (Gerz case p. 50; reference p. 115)

John Wiley & Sons, Ltd.
   (Mindess case p. 56; reference p. 117)

Dr. Harvey Mindess
   (cartoon, p. 58)

Rational Living
   (Ellis cases pp. 62–63; reference p. 114)

William Alanson White Foundation, Inc.
   (Nelson case p. 65; reference p. 117)

Nursing Publications, Inc.
   (Roncoli case p. 67; reference p. 118)

Psychotherapy: Theory, Research & Practice
   (Greenwald case p. 68; reference p. 115)

Mr. Frank Farrelly, Dr. Jeffrey Brandsma, & Meta Publications, Inc.
   (cases pp. 71 & 73; reference p. 114)

Dr. Harold F. Searles & *International Journal of Psychoanalysis*
   (case p. 86; reference p. 119)

American Journal of Psychoanalysis
   (Coleman case p. 69; reference p. 114)

American Journal of Psychotherapy
   (Shaw case p. 99; reference p. 119)

Social Casework
   (Orfanidis case p. 100; reference p. 118)

Dr. Salvador Minuchin & Harvard University Press
   (case p. 102; reference p. 117)

Family Process
   (Zuk case p. 105; reference p. 120)

British Journal of Medical Psychology
   (Bloch, Browning, & McGrath cases pp. 107 & 109; reference
   p. 114)

Contents

Chapter 1

Introduction

      A front-page column in a local newspaper publicized my work on this project while it was still in its early stages. The newspaper story prompted about 25 phone calls and letters from the public during the next two weeks. All of these reactions were positive; those that came from current and former psychotherapy clients usually included an "it's about time" sort of statement.

      Few of my academic and professional colleagues commented on the story at all; those who did so were polite or ambivalent. A week after the story appeared, one colleague related that some of his clients had brought up the article in their therapy sessions with him. When I asked how these discussions had gone, he smiled and said facetiously "It's all grist for the mill." Another colleague good-naturedly dubbed me the Good Humor Man: he seemed to be implying that humor in psychotherapy tastes good but has little nutritional value. I was also approached by an advanced psychiatry resident who "confessed" to me that she and her clients often shared humor and laughter in their sessions. During supervision hours she usually played down or deleted these humorous incidents because she was apprehensive about her supervisor's response—and uncertain whether humor belonged in psychotherapy at all.

The skepticism implicit in the reactions of my colleagues is understandable in light of the destructive impact which critical humor can have. But the reaction of the public is also valid: humor can serve as a potent force in change processes and has a place within the psychotherapeutic relationship as it does in all other forms of human relationships. These latter views have been endorsed by Albert Ellis, Harold Greenwald, and other psychotherapists who have drawn overflow crowds to symposia on the subject at American Psychological Association conventions. But in researching the topic one finds a scant and scattered literature. This literature can be summarized as 15 years of pro-and-con debate, often with repetitive lists of "dos and don'ts," "whens and when-nots." Frequently, the same point is made in several theoretical languages without any connections being drawn among them. Seldom is there an analysis and synthesis of the role that humor plays in relationships, or how humor functions in persuasion and attitude change as satirists and cartoonists have used it for centuries.

This monograph seeks to achieve an analysis and synthesis of humor in psychotherapy with an attitude of respect and unstable neutrality. It focuses primarily upon dyadic psychotherapy for, as will be discussed later, humor and laughter within a dyad have different meanings and implications than when they occur within a group that includes a participating or observing audience as well as a sender and a receiver.

Few published papers on the topic of humor and psychotherapy predate 1970. In part this reflects a longstanding taboo in the behavioral sciences which has withheld attention from other pleasure phenomena, such as love, ecstasy, and success (Allport, 1950; Chapman & Foot, 1976). Keith-Spiegel (1969) estimated that "humor-related behavior exceeds all other types of emotional behaviors combined . . . by ten or more times." In fact, Killinger (1976) reported laughter and nonlaughter humor to be a high frequency event in her study of audiotapes of adult psychotherapy. Nevertheless, mere allusions to laughter and humor are rare in books about psychotherapy and counseling; separate "laughter" and "humor" entries in the indices of such books are virtually nonexistent.

Among the three philosophical mainstreams of modern psychotherapeutic practice, psychoanalysis has ignored humor the least. Sigmund Freud's two treatises on humor are well known; his ambivalent and shifting attitudes toward the subject are not. In *Jokes and Their Relation to the Unconscious* (1905), Freud articulates the workings of humor (particularly the "tendentious" variety involving sexual or aggressive content) as a drive derivative or defense mechanism with the maladaptive connotations customarily associated with such concepts. In "Humour" (1928) he described conditions under which similar humor mechanisms signify "something fine and elevating:"

> Obviously, what is fine about it is the triumph of narcissism, the ego's victorious assertion of its own invulnerability. It refuses to be hurt by the arrows of reality or to be compelled to suffer. It insists that it is impervious to wounds dealt by the outside world, in fact, that these are merely occasions for affording it pleasure. (p. 217)

In this statement Freud's concepts of humor as both distorting reality and transcending it are inseparable. This dilemma (for psychoanalysis at least) is further complicated by the fact that Freud twice made depreciating comments about his work on humor (see James Strachey's Preface to *Jokes and Their Relation to the Unconscious*). Finally, there is not a single allusion in Freud's writings on the conduct of treatment to the analyst's being humorous during the session. Yet Loewenstein (1958) described it as common knowledge that Freud himself used jokes when analyzing.

This inconsistent attitude continued after Freud. Kris (1938) and Reik (1949) are two prominent psychoanalysts who have written about the adaptive strengths epitomized in humor; neither discussed any relevant role that humor may play in treatment. Maurice Grotjahn (1949) was the first psychoanalyst to espouse humor as a therapeutic vehicle and still retain a reputation of eminence among his colleagues (see Mendel, 1970). Still, the most widely cited paper in this area by a psychoanalyst is Lawrence Kubie's (1971) "The Destructive Potential of Humor in Psychotherapy." Interestingly, Kubie first presented the paper to a colloquium honoring Dr. Grotjahn.

In the first two decades of the behavior therapy tradition (1950–70) there is not a single allusion to humor in that literature. A recent increase of interest in humor and psychotherapy can be traced to the humanistic tradition; yet Carl Rogers, the father-figure of this movement, has never alluded to humor in

his many writings on client-centered therapy. The only documented response of Rogers to the place of humor in therapy
emerged in a panel discussion involving Rogers, Harold Greenwald, and several other prominent therapists who had been
discussing their various approaches. Greenwald (1975) recalls:

> I said that I thought psychotherapy should be fun. When
> I said it, I was sitting close to Carl Rogers. I saw the red start at
> his collar and spread up and go over his face, and finally he burst
> out, "I think it's hard work, and if you think it's fun, then to hell
> with you." (p. 114)

Obviously, there is more than pleasure taboo underlying
these attitudes. Consider that the pioneers within each school of
thought were earnestly seeking methods to alleviate human
pain and suffering—and that all espoused the scientific
method. As their ideas gained recognition, students and adherents gravitated to them and bestowed an aura of solemn admiration upon their work. Theoretical "camps" developed whose
early behavior toward each other displayed a rigidity and eth-
nocentrism more commonly associated with religions and cults.
Psychotherapy has thus evolved as a hybrid of science and religion; these are two areas of human endeavor with which humor
is seldom compatible.

Recently, however, there has been a proliferation of new
therapy systems and styles and an increased spirt of eclecticism.
Behavior therapy has become cognitive (e.g., Meichenbaum,
1977) and psychoanalysis has spawned a variety of approaches
that are brief and focal in nature (e.g., Malan, 1976). Attention
is being devoted to the integration of these seemingly diverse
theoretical approaches (e.g., Wachtel, 1977). Outcome research
generally fails to endorse one theoretical orientation over another. Teachers and writers in the field place less emphasis on
theoretical orthodoxy than they did 25 years ago. Instead they
call for practitioners who are empathic, spontaneous, flexible,
and creative. These qualities are also the essence of effective
humor; thus it becomes difficult to argue that psychotherapists
must leave their sense of humor outside the office door to be
effective. On the other hand, humor must be viewed as a trans-
actional process involving a sender and a receiver and not as a
"thing" that exists independently of the participants. A client in
pain may be an ill-suited participant no matter how skillful a
therapist is with humorous interventions.

Another impetus behind humor's late emergence as a force in therapeutic change was the publication of Norman Cousins' *Anatomy of an Illness* in 1979. Cousins, a renowned journalist and editor of *Saturday Review*, contracted a rare and "incurable" collagen disease while on assignment in the Soviet Union. His autobiograhical book describes his road to recovery from the disease, a recovery which he attributes in large part to massive doses of vitamin C and massive doses of laughter (the latter were "administered" by viewing Marx Brothers movies and other comedies from his hospital bed). Cousins' interpretation of his cure is couched in cautious language; nevertheless, the book has been widely read in both lay and professional circles, and Cousins continues to be in great demand as a lecturer on the merits of holistic health. *Anatomy of an Illness* has subsequently been followed by a spate of self-help-through-humor books, the introduction of humor into stress management programs and workshops, and an article in *Prevention Magazine* (December, 1982) devoted to the prophylactic value of humor.

Taken together, these influences suggest that the professional *zeitgeist* is ripe for a book of this kind.

This monograph is addressed to psychotherapists of all experience levels and theoretical persuasions who have encountered, shared, or generated humor in their sessions and seldom given it much thought. It seeks to provide a broad base of knowledge about humor, its benefits, and its dangers. Its intent is to educate rather than advocate or dissuade.

If my experience is typical, therapists who grow more self-conscious of humor will initially experience minor disruptions in the flow of their work. Their participation in the comic relief which occasional humorous interludes provide will be less full. These side effects are unavoidable but also short-lived. For while there are many subtleties and complexities inherent to humor-tinged interactions, these appear finite in number. All of us have encountered these various facets of humor in other relationships if not in the practice of psychotherapy. Self-consciousness about humor need be only temporary and non-obtrusive; understanding its implications quickly becomes second nature and takes up residence in "the third ear." One soon cultivates a sense of when a humorous interlude should be made a focus of the therapy and of when it is best left in the background. And one acquires a new dimension upon which to assess one's clients and their progress toward therapeutic goals. At the present time in my practice there is one client with whom I share humor as often as possible; another whose constant efforts to generate humor are discouraged; and others with whom infrequent humor is appreciated in its own right *and* for the light it sheds upon where the person is at a given time and where the person is likely to be moving in the near future. I have little doubt that these clients experience and understand my workings as a therapist in a similar fashion.

Professional comedians have often criticized behavioral scientists who study humor by arguing that the phenomenon is destroyed by the process of scrutinizing it. This is certainly the case when humor is studied rather than experienced, when its observer strives for detachment and objectivity. In psychotherapy, however, the therapist constantly mingles the subjective with the objective; mingles involvement with detachment; is both a participant and an observer. Scrutinizing humor while sharing in it need not detract from the experience and may ultimately enhance it. Connoisseurs of art, music, wine, and so on do not lose their ability to appreciate their objets d'art after developing an educated understanding of them. So it is with humor, which has been called the art form of every man.

There are intrinsic difficulties in writing about humor in psychotherapy. Foremost is the paradox of its "use." When discussed as a technique, humor connotes something planned and calculated—yet spontaneity is the essence of all effective humor. The many humorous interventions discussed in this book vary in the degree of forethought involved. At one extreme, for example, some psychoanalysts have recommended interpreting unconscious conflicts to clients through time-honored jokes. Viktor Frankl's use of humor in paradoxical intention follows a standardized, even stereotypical formula. Nevertheless, in the majority of instances it is clear that therapeutic humor arises from the therapist's spontaneous sense of humor rather than from a prearranged plan to use humor.

Unfortunately, in writing about these humorous interludes, authors include conventional "introduction" and "discussion" sections which relate humor to prevailing concepts and methods. This helps to bestow some credibilty to an intervention mode that has long been in disrepute; the cost associated with this benefit is that the spontaneity factor is buried and

humor is portrayed as an element of the therapist's arma-
mentarium rather than an interactional dynamic. For this reason I have avoided discussing the "uses of humor" whenever
possible in favor of "applying one's sense of humor to some
useful end." The difference between these two character-
izations is not simply semantic.

A related problem evolves from the critical incident
method adopted here to illustrate and amplify certain points. In
written form these clinical vignettes can never be adequately
captured in their context. A central thesis of this monograph is
that state-of-the-relationship factors and play signals are as important as humor content in generating a humorous effect.
Authors vary in the amount of context they supply when reporting humorous vignettes; in some cases the reader will have
difficulty in discerning any humor to them at all. Where relevant context features are lacking, I have inserted my own inferences and speculations as to likely context factors which were
operative at the time. In instances where it is still difficult to
grasp the humor of a situation, the reader must join me in
taking the author at his/her word. We have all been in situations
where retelling a joke or recounting a funny experience has
fallen flat and we have been left to conclude that "you had to be
there the first time to appreciate it."

The premise upon which this monograph is based is that
humor in psychotherapy has short-term and long-term effects
which can be distinguished. The short-term effects are signaled
by the tension reduction, mirth, and other emotional responses
which are the immediate sequelae to any effective humor. These
have been studied and articulated by philosophers and scientists who have examined humor outside of the psychotherapy
situation (Chapter 2).

With some exceptions, humor has been conceived as having moment-to-moment tactical benefits in therapy rather than
as an overall strategy or goal. On the one hand, it can facilitate
a client's movement into a problem upon which the humor is
built (Chapter 3); on the other, it can promote the client's psychological distance away from the problem at hand (Chapter 4).
Which of these two opposing ends is achieved depends upon the
therapist-client interaction prior and subsequent to the occurrence of the humorous interlude.

The long-term effects of humor (whether considered as
isolated instances or collectively) are to shape, define, and

change the relationship of the participants. Hostile, sarcastic, and put-down humor has been described as promoting insight into a problem or detachment away from a problem in many different psychotherapy systems (Chapter 5). The fact that such aggressive humor can achieve therapeutic ends without re-sulting in the client's unilateral termination attests to re-lationship factors which mitigate the expected negative con-sequences of the therapist's attack. On the other hand, Freud's concept of veiled aggression may apply in circumstances where these relationship factors do not exist. The therapist then may blindly (or otherwise) tyrannize a client under the guise of help-ful humor. In these and other circumstances humor in psycho-therapy has clear destructive potential (Chapter 6).

Group and family settings alter the meaning and impli-cations of humor dramatically (Chapter 7). While these ther-apeutic modalities have been less well studied with respect to humor, it will be made clear that humor serves different func-tions within them than it does in dyadic psychotherapy.

Chapter 2

Concepts of Humor

          The nature of humor has been addressed by many of the great thinkers in the history of philosophy and science; Plato, Aristotle, Descartes, Hobbes, Kant, Schopenhauer, Darwin, Freud, Spencer, and Piaget are the best known. If one adds the contributions of many others, scores of humor theories have been generated. Keith-Spiegel (1972) has summarized the majority of these theories and grouped them into eight broad categories (evolution, superiority, incongruity, surprise, ambivalence, relief, configurational, and psychoanalytic). Each theory seems to have its hands on a part of the humor phenomenon, but none has humor's essence firmly in grasp.

          There have also been attempts to specify discrete kinds of humor: most lists include cartoon, clowning, comedy, farce, jest, joke, parody, pun, riddle, ridicule, sarcasm, satire, and slapstick. As Sully (1902) observed about humor, "hardly a word in the language—and it seems to be exclusively an English word—would be harder to define with scientific precision than this familiar one" (p. 297). McGhee (1979) has suggested that the number of different types of humor is "limited only by our own capacity to make distinctions between humorous events" (p. 8).

Trying to capture the essence of humor is like trying to define "learning." We can agree in our recognition of when it occurs, and we know when humor has been effective and when it has failed. We can further identify and distinguish between lower forms of humor (puns, riddles) and higher forms (sophisticated allusions, double entendrés). Yet we remain hard pressed to say what humor is.

The approach adopted here in organizing the growing body of knowledge about humor views it as an intervening variable rather than as a discrete phenomenon or "thing." A definition of humor is not attempted; rather, humor is conceived as a putative link between certain classes of responses and certain classes of stimuli that occurs under certain contextual conditions.

The humor response

Humor responses range from the mild, perhaps barely observable sense of amusement and mirth through the smile to the violent physiological reaction known as laughter. To be considered as evidence of genuine humor, smiling and laughter must be less than voluntary; they are emotional reactions that are evoked rather than emitted. Consider how learning material may be taken in, rehearsed in rote fashion, and regurgitated to give the false impression that true learning has taken place. Similarly, smiling and laughter may be rote when the relationship between sender and receiver demands it (e.g., a superior-subordinate relationship) or there is a social contagion effect among a group of humor receivers.

The neurophysiology of smiling and laughter has not been thoroughly studied. The smile involves innervation of muscular responses through the facial nerve; its neuropsychological concomitants elude detection by current scientific methods and are presumably subtle. The smile initially appears during the first week of life when the neonate is asleep; within two weeks an infant will smile during wakeful, nonalert states, typically after feeding (McGhee, 1979). This is a sign of physiological well-being as it is not associated with external stimuli. The first alert smile to an external stimulus occurs at the end of the first month, usually to a mother figure. Some theorists have interpreted this to be a social smile signaling the onset of an emotional bonding process between mother and child. Such an interpretation attributes a dubious complexity to infant psychology. More than likely, these early, alert smiles denote the infant's initial recognition of something with regularity and repeatability in an otherwise chaotic visual world. Sensing regularity and repeatability is incongruous with the infant's brief life experience and, as McGhee (1979) has hinted, suggests that a sense of humor may develop before a "sense of mother." Mother typically prompts and/or responds to her infant's smile with a smile of her own. From this smile interchange, arising from vastly different motivational sources in mother and child, a bonding language is formed and the social smile splits off from the humorous smile in terms of its sources and meanings.

Laughter first appears in the fourth or fifth month (Washburn, 1929). Typically, the initial stimulus is tactile; visual and social stimuli evoke laughter shortly thereafter. Tactile stimulation anywhere on the infant's body can evoke laughter initially. The number and range of sensitive body areas decreases with age—as the infant's life experiences with tactile stimulation increase, its novelty (incongruity with previous experience) decreases.

Tickled laughter is generally viewed as a phenomenon grounded in neurophysiology (Stearns, 1972). But there is always a social basis to tickling—it is difficult, if not impossible, to tickle oneself effectively. It is also worth noting that the areas where older children and adults are most prone to tickling—underarms, soles of the feet, sexual areas—are areas that seldom receive focal tactile stimulation. The laughter evoked by tickling may thus be grounded in a simultaneous acknowledgement and denial of an attack. The fact that it is a vigorous stimulation of seldom exposed, seldom stimulated areas constitutes an attack; if it is launched by a significant other with whom the victim generally feels safe, this constitutes reason to deny an attack. In addition to neurophysiology, then, tickling entails incongruity and paradox.

The neurophysiology of laughter is better understood than that of the smile (e.g., Stearns, 1972). The upheaval of normal respiratory patterns, laughter's hallmark, is set in motion by the vagus nerve. The pleasure resides in the quick discharge of tension and energy through the musculature of the face and abdomen. There are circumstances when laughter is not so pleasurably experienced; persons with multiple sclerosis and other forms of brain disease may show symptoms of pathological laughter without an accompanying sense of pleasure or mirth (Stearns, 1972; Goldstein, 1982).

Most research interest in humor responses has been concentrated upon underlying autonomic nervous system changes rather than the overt manifestations of humor in the smile and the laugh. Changes in heart rate, respiration, the galvanic skin response, blood pressure, lacrimation, etc. are typical accompaniments of laughter. The impetus for this work was Berlyne's (1960, 1972) theory linking curiosity, play, art appreciation, humor, and other hedonic experiences with changes in autonomic nervous system arousal. The novel, the incongruous, the unexpected stimulus poses a challenge to the person's information-processing capacities. Cognitive dissonance is created; autonomic arousal is part of the initial response to this disruption of normal adaptational functioning ("arousal boost").

Autonomic arousal appears to be a necessary condition for the humor experience. For example, Schachter and Wheeler (1962) reported that their subjects who were injected with epinephrine showed greater enjoyment during a humorous movie than subjects who were injected with a saline solution. A third group of subjects, who were injected with a tranquilizer, enjoyed the movie least of all. Another method of studying arousal and humor is to monitor autonomic nervous system functions while subjects are exposed to humor stimuli (e.g., Langevin & Day, 1972; Goldstein, Harman, McGhee, & Karasik, 1975). The results of such studies are neither straightforward nor consistent; some suggest that the pleasure of humor is grounded solely in an arousal boost while others support the concept of an "arousal jag." An arousal jag consists of an initial arousal boost when the puzzle of the humor stimulus is confronted, followed by a sudden drop in arousal when the puzzle solution (the "punchline") is grasped.

Emotional arousal is not a sufficient condition for the pleasure of humor: the physiological patterns of arousal during humor are not qualitatively different from those of other emotional states. For humor to occur, (1) its originator must generate play signals (McGhee, 1979) to predispose receiver(s) to a playful frame of mind, (2) the social environment must be appropriate for playing, and (3) the play stimulus must possess certain characteristics.

The humor stimulus

The bulk of philosophical and scientific work on the nature of humor has evolved from studying humor stimuli and attempting to explain how such stimuli are capable of evoking such a prominent psychosomatic response. Most everyday humor experiences involve some dimension of verbal language and thought; less commonly, humor can be purely visual as in captionless cartoons. Speeding up soundless motion pictures typically creates humor in a manner by which Charlie Chaplin and Keystone Cop movies still amuse. The humor of clowns and mimes is also exclusively visual. Tickling can be viewed as a form of tactile humor; the nonlanguage sounds of the robot R2D2 from the *Star Wars* films is an example of auditory humor. We commonly hear people speaking of substances smelling or tasting "funny." Finally, in an ingenious experiment, Nerhardt (1970) reported that he was able to regularly induce laughter in experimental subjects who were doing a nonverbal weight lifting task. After lifting a monotonous series of weights of approximately equal heaviness, subjects broke into laughter when the next weight was either much heavier or much lighter than those earlier in the series. This unusual form of psychophysical humor further suggests that humor can be induced through all perceptual modalities.

In reviewing the range of theories that attempt to explain why certain stimuli evoke mirth or amusement, reference will be made to the following joke:

Question: What is the difference between herpes and true love?
Answer: Herpes lasts forever.

Cognitive theories. Most cognitive models of humor emphasize qualities of the stimulus structure rather than the stimulus content. In the example above there are a number of incongruous or unexpected features to the communication. The receiver is first posed the implicit premise that herpes and true love have many things in common. Aside from their connection with sexual intercourse they would appear to have little in common. As ideas or concepts they make for strange bedfellows; they are an incongruous or unexpected combination. Remove the phrase "true love" and substitute "gonorrhea" and the question may serve as a short essay question for a high school sex education class.

But, posed with this riddle, the receiver is asked to suspend normal logical and adaptational thought processes and adopt an apples = oranges frame of mind. The receiver can likely think of many ways that the two ideas are different, but the wording of the question suggests only one is the correct answer. When the punchline appears, the receiver finds that the answer is equally incongruous to the premise. "Lasts Forever" in fact may be one of the few ways in which the two ideas can be thought of as *similar* rather than different (at least until a cure for herpes is achieved). Thus the question and answer are both absurd, but there is a consistency to the illogic: the question implies that two very different things are highly similar, and the answer balances with one of few areas of similarity being proposed as their only difference.

Humorous incongruity can take many forms—in the pun or the double entendré, for example, two meaning senses of the same word or phrase coexist and compete. The resulting vacillation in the receiver's mind disrupts the normal flow of information processing; but the disruption is a mild one and is experienced as a pleasant change of pace. For humor to occur the degree of incongruity present must be optimal. If there is too little, it will not be sufficient to disrupt the normal flow of thought and will either go unnoticed or be experienced as disappointing (thus we "groan" upon hearing a less than clever pun). Most humor stimuli lose their amusement potential after the first presentation because once the incongruity is solved it ceases to pose a puzzle and challenge to the receiver's cognitive abilities. Too much incongruity evokes concentration and curiosity behavior—in extreme forms anxiety, panic, perhaps psychosis. Humorous incongruity lies between these two extremes. Its resolution must involve some effort but not too much. The importance of correct timing to the punchline of a joke highlights how the logistics of tension building and its resolution are crucial in generating a sense of amusement.

Incongruity is the dominant force in children's humor, and the kinds of humor preferred by children at various ages reflect different stages of cognitive development. The infant's delight with a peekaboo game occurs at a time when s/he is actively grappling with the concept that objects continue to exist when they cannot be perceived. Rhymes appeal to the older child who struggles with the mastery of language: sensing regularity and rhythm in language is a delight to one who previously perceived language as difficult and chaotic. Puns have appeal to the primary school child as s/he first learns that words can have more than one meaning. Jokes such as the following one:

Pizza Man: Would you like your pizza cut into four or six pieces?

Customer: Six pieces please. I'm extra hungry today.

appeal to the older child with dawning awareness of Piagetian conservation principles. A mastery-through-play motive underlies all humor—for children, it is predominantly the slow and gradual mastery of thought and language patterns that are habitual to the adult.

Motivational theories.   For adults, incongruity is a necessary but not sufficient condition to induce laughter and mirth. In addition to an incongruous meaning structure, humor stimuli which are effective with adults often involve sexual or aggressive content. In the herpes-true love example, the theme of sexual promiscuity contributes prominently to amusement value.

Freud (1905) viewed sexual and aggressive humor as a release valve of the ego in its struggle to manage libidinal drives. This "tendentious" humor, as he termed it, functions like a defense mechanism, and the acute, fleeting pleasure of amusement occurs because an impulse has been expressed that otherwise would have been repressed or induced superego punishment. Freud's hydraulic model of tendentious humor has considerable intuitive appeal, and the prominence of sexual and aggressive content in adult interactions and entertainment calls for some such explanation.

It may be more profitable and palatable to those who reject Freud's drive concept to view tendentious humor in its process aspects (the violation of a social taboo) rather than its specific content aspects of sex and aggression. In normal, adaptive functioning within society, the adult is forced to inhibit sexual urges and moderate aggressive responses to frustration for the welfare of the societal group and the maintenance of its order. The opportunity to violate social mores in a play setting such as humor is then inherently pleasurable—just as daydreams and achievement fantasies provide relief from other kinds of personal dissatisfactions. Humor is a more ambitious outlet, however, because it invites another to join and share in the play. One advantage of changing from a drive reduction model to a taboo violation perspective is the parallel that appears with cognitive theories of humor. Alford (1982) has observed that incongruity structures violate principles of logic (thought); taboo content violates principles of conduct (behavior). Interestingly, the herpes-true love joke embraces a theme that reinforces social strictures against promiscuity even as the taboo topic is breached. "Herpes lasts forever" suggests a cruel punishment bequeathed to the violator. The joke thus completes a crime and punishment cycle.

Another motivational aspect of the joke's content is the implication that "true love does not last forever." This cynical attitude toward what is generally viewed as a lofty, social value taps the disappointments and frustrations that persons universally experience in pursuing the idealized goal of "true love." Viewing a painful experience in this detached, cynical way provides a sense of mastery over it. Existentialists have emphasized this role of humor in distancing oneself from experience in order to master it from a different perspective. A frequently cited example of existential humor is the "no thanks, I just quit" response of the condemned prisoner who is offered a cigarette before being executed.

A final amusement feature shown by effective humor stimuli is salience (Goldstein, Suls, and Anthony, 1972). Salience refers to a mental set established in a receiver to perceive certain events as funny. For example, I heard the herpes-true love joke told by three unconnected individuals in three different American cities during the summer of 1982. Its spread and appeal at that time was generated by a cover story in a national news magazine the previous spring announcing herpes as a disease that had reached epidemic proportions in the United States.[1] Certain comedians are well known for their skill with topical humor that addresses knowledge and concerns fresh in the minds of their audiences. Johnny Carson's nightly monologue is a prime example of this influence of content salience.

---

[1] In the summer of 1983, AIDS was a more topical sexual disease than herpes; thus AIDS jokes became popular and herpes jokes were heard less frequently.

The humor context

Whether or not a given stimulus will evoke a humor response depends heavily upon its social context. The herpes-true love joke was an effective one in a tavern and again at a cocktail party. But told in the vestibule of a church it would surely offend someone. Many work settings are similarly not conducive to laughter.

Berlyne (1972) has emphasized that for humor to be effective the receiver must be in a playful frame of mind. Apter and Smith (1977) have distinguished between telic and paratelic states of mind: in the telic state an individual is goal-oriented and the processing of experience is in the service of reaching some goal. Humor is associated with the paratelic state in which mental activity is experienced and enjoyed for its own sake, not in the service of some adaptional goal. Kris (1938) and other psychoanalytic authors have viewed humor as an instance of regression by the ego that is neither pathological nor maladaptive.

However conceived, it is clear that to generate or appreciate humor one must be able to shift to a special mental perspective. To accomplish this, the sender of humor typically prepares the receiver by first issuing a "play signal" (McGhee, 1979). This serves as a cue, a prompt, a priming for the humor stimulus that is to come. It may be a sudden lilt in the sender's voice, a change in facial expression or body language, or even an announcement that "I heard a good one that other day at a party . . ." At times the setting itself functions as a play signal— as when a nightclub advertises the appearance of a comedian. Or it may be the laughter responses of a group of recipients which tells the individual how to process the humor stimulus and how to respond. The social contagiousness of laughter is well known—the "canned laughter" tracks that are added to the audio portions of television comedies represent an attempt to capitalize upon laughter's contagiousness and to convince viewers that certain interactions and communications are funny.

The play signal thus functions as an invitation from sender to receiver to suspend the normal "work" of adaptation and enjoy a brief play period. The invitation is not always accepted, or may be accepted provisionally and then refused. Herpes-true love would certainly alienate a herpes victim; and perhaps oth-

ers in an acute state of "true love." Ethnic jokes typically offend
members of the ethnic group being disparaged; sexual jokes
may be effective in a male-male dyad or within a female-female
dyad, but not in a male-female dyad.

The fate of the play signal and ultimately of the humor
itself thus rests also upon the relationship between the sender
and receiver. The violation of societal taboos against the expression of sexuality and hostility sets the dyad apart from society
when the receiver accepts the invitation to play. Sender and
receiver form an in-group, the rest of the social world an out-
group. Freud's view of disparagement humor as an outlet for
pent-up aggression may be shortsighted; according to Martineau (1972) the more important function of disparagement
humor is to solidify the alliance of the in-group and enhance its
morale. Should the sender unwittingly invite a receiver who
maintains stronger alliances with the targeted victim or value
than with the sender, the sender-receiver relationship is threatened. It encourages open conflict and hostility between sender
and receiver; any positive relationship between them that had
been previously established moves toward demoralization and
disintegration.

Martineau's theory of the social functions of humor attempts to explain the ubiquity of ethnic humor. It also applies
to political humor and sexual humor that demeans one of the
sexes. In some contexts "misery loves company" is a motivational source for the humor: e.g., two taxpayers caustically
wisecracking about their shared fate shortly after a change of
political administrations or two high school boys ridiculing the
shortcomings of a girl who refused to go out on a date with
either of them. In other cases—when the disparagement theme
is less acute, less immediate, or less salient—the sender's humor
may be motivated by a desire to establish or change ground
rules in the relationship with the receiver. The sender may be
probing whether the receiver shares values and attitudes with
respect to a particular issue. In the first humorous breach of
a taboo, the sender is conveying a message that s/he would like
to make room for more intimacy within the dyad. In other
instances the sender may wish to initiate a serious discussion
of a controversial subject with an initial assurance of safety
from attack. Herpes-true love, for example, may serve as overture humor when a sender wishes to explore sexual relationships. Such humor can serve breaking-the-ice functions; be-

cause it is done under the auspices of play it provides for an easy retreat.

In articulating these and other social functions of humor, Kane, Suls, and Tedeschi (1977) point out the unique characteristics of humor in the service of in-group formation and intimacy probe: its quality of "play" and its essential ambiguity allow the sender to decommit and save face if the play signal is refused or the humor is not appreciated. "I was only joking" is a disclaimer we have all been forced to make at one time or another when a quip or one-liner fails to amuse. The receiver's response to this temporizing provides the sender with some direction to pursue in further defining the relationship (or repairing it if need be). The receiver, for example, might say "Don't worry about it," indicating that the breach of taboo was not a serious offense and the relationship need not disintegrate. The receiver may decline comment and change the subject, suggesting that the offense has been a serious one but as long as the particular taboo violated is not addressed again, the relationship has some future. Or the receiver may inform the sender that "A good friend of mine contracted herpes," in which case the receiver is accepting the intimacy invitation but offering a change of ground rules. If the sender-receiver relationship is not antagonistic, the receiver will not retaliate as if to an attack. For there is always a playful quality to the vehicle of humor, irrespective of content; its illogic, its psychotic thought structure provides a built-in decommitment theme that generalizes to its content.

When the sender-receiver relationship is defined as antagonistic, disparagement humor takes on saber-rattling functions. If the receiver laughs it will have a canned quality and represent a temporizing response. The receiver may also retaliate with a second insult joke—if there is a nonaligned audience whose presence reinforces social taboos against open aggression, sender and receiver may continue in a one-upmanship exchange of humor blows with the audience laughter volume conveying the score. In the absence of contextual factors upholding the aggression taboo, open hostility and violence may emerge. The decommitment features associated with play signals and incongruous thought structure are thus modified by contextual forces.

Clever incongruity, keenness in timing, and other logistic dimensions are the structural aspects of humor that render it a potent vehicle in persuasion and attitude change. The inherent pleasure provided by such play to the receiver bestows intellectual prowess upon the sender. In turn this creates a halo effect upon the message and the sender who conveys it. The surrealistic ambiguity of humor also provides decommitment options; thus political satirists and cartoonists throughout history have been both powerful and elusive adversaries to governments in struggles over political and social reforms.

When a high degree of intimacy is already established in a relationship, the limits of appropriate humor expand as do the number and severity of taboos which may be violated in safety. Disparagement humor in which the sender attacks the receiver may become a token of affection; if the same insult were delivered by a person perceived as outside of the intimacy circle it would constitute an attack. Radcliffe-Brown (1940) first described such joking relationships among African tribes in which one person might be "required" to tease and antagonize another and the victim "required" to take no offense. A ritualized American example of disparagement humor as tribute is the celebrity roast. It began as a semiregular television special hosted by Dean Martin in the late 1960s; today it is an event that is often staged locally as an after-dinner entertainment at fund-raising banquets. The script of the roast dictates that the celebrity person being honored sit beside the speaker's dais while a parade of friends, admirers, and other celebrities take turns at the dais insulting the person by exaggerating the celebrity's foibles and satirizing the victim's personality traits to howls of laughter from an admiring audience. The roast victim typically laughs as hard as anyone at the character assassination; often the celebrity is handed the microphone at the end of the event and humorously assassinates the characters of those who had been attacking earlier. The event typically ends with a genuine standing ovation for the roast victim. This represents a collective undoing that further negates the disparagement humor that the victim has received and transforms it to an affirmation of admiration and esteem.

Taken as a group, these social phenomena indicate that hostile, put-down, and disparagement humor can not be characterized simply as aggression outlets. When viewed in the light of the prevailing relationships among the senders, receivers, and targets of such humor, multiple layers of meaning to such humor emerge.

Humor and adjustment

Cousins' (1979) testimonial to the healing powers of laughter is only the most recent rendition of the old adage "laughter is the best medicine." Physicians since the 13th century have prescribed laughter as a means of maintaining healthy bodily functions and avoiding illness (see Goldstein, 1982). The release of muscular tension and the brief, strenuous exercise it entails enhance physiological health. Cousins has further speculated that laughter causes the release of endorphins (the body's analgesic-anesthetic hormone) into the bloodstream.

The beneficial psychological consequences of laughter and humor are evident in studies of educational processes. Zillmann et al (1980), for example, showed that the acquisition of new information is facilitated when an element of humor is injected into the learning content. The time-honored success and appeal of such educational television shows as "Sesame Street" can be attributed to their heavy use of humor and other forms of imaginative play. Skilled public speakers and orators sprinkle their presentations with humor to maximize audience attention. Ronald Reagan's ready wit compared favorably to Jimmy Carter's constant solemnity during the 1980 presidential debate. This certainly contributed to Reagan's unofficial victory in the debate.

The capacity to both produce humor and appreciate it has been positively correlated with measures of intelligence (e.g., Getzels & Jackson, 1962) and empathy (e.g., Roberts & Johnson, 1957). Koestler (1964) discusses humor as a special subclass of creativity and research has supported an association between humor and varied measures of creative behavior (Rouff, 1975; Verma, 1981; Ziv, 1983). In a review article, Hickson (1977) reported that self-actualization theorists including Gordon Allport, Combs and Snygg, Abraham Maslow, and Carl Rogers have endorsed the sense of humor as a cardinal trait of the fully functioning person, but like their psychoanalyst counterparts, none has articulated a role for humor in psychotherapy. There have been isolated research reports documenting a relationship between humor and mental health (e.g., O'Connell, 1960), but this promising line of research has been hampered by difficulties defining and measuring the elusive concepts involved.

One particular form of humor that has been repeatedly discussed in conjunction with coping behavior is that in which the sender of humor is also the victim of a joke. In its mildest form self-directed humor may involve making light of one's misfortunes by taking what Monro (1951) called the "god's eye view:" for example, a friend recently ended a morbid account of her child custody and property settlement battles in court with her ex-husband by exclaiming, "My divorce—that's one thing they can never take away from me!" It is this kind of humor that Freud alluded to as both distorting and transcending reality.

Self-disparagement humor, in which the sender of the humor attacks the self (rather than events befalling the self), has also been viewed as a coping behavior (Mindess, 1971). Goldstein (1976) conceives the dynamics this way:

> It is possible, then, to diminish one's inadequacies . . . by jesting, about them. The jest makes the inadequacies themselves appear laughable. It remains unclear whether such joking helps people overcome whatever real inadequacies may exist, but for the moment the jokes place shortcomings on an objective level so that they become temporarily part of the non-self, objects to be toyed with. This objectification of one's weaknesses makes them appear either unreal, by exaggeration, or trivial, by comparison with a larger-than-life object or concept. (p. 110)

In support of this position, Rule (1977) has provided some pilot study evidence that self-disparagement humor leads to increased self-esteem. Self-ridicule also has a positive effect on others by uplifting them in the process of downing oneself or by inviting others to provide sympathy, support, or other gestures of affiliation. Rodney Dangerfield is a popular comedian who earns his living almost exclusively through self-depreciation.

But self-disparagement can be viewed in more neutral terms when it is frequent, stereotyped, or a chronic style of life. It can serve self-protective functions—"I'll attack myself before you have a chance to do so." As an interpersonal tactic this enables the sender-victim to neutralize a potential critic, perhaps even transform the critic into a sympathetic admirer. Wilson (1979) has drawn further inferences about self-abusing humor:

> This serves a passive, peaceful resistance; for although the joker expresses self-criticism, he does not intend to change his characteristics. He is saying "I'm funny, but I like myself, and shall stay as I am." . . . for the joke may be interpreted as being

apologetically ingratiating, whilst expressing a hidden defiance."
(p. 147)

Self-ridicule as a style of life may also connote excessive
needs for attention. Fisher and Fisher (1981) found this a
prominent feature in the family dynamics of a series of
"schlemiel" children who were presented to them for evaluation
and treatment because of constant antics that led to poor school
performance and behavioral problems. Many cultures, prim-
itive and otherwise, have evolved institutionalized roles for self-
abasement humor: the clown, the fool, the jester, the Cheyenne
contrary. These "professionals" usually adopt a self-ridiculing
appearance to match their behavior. While they serve important
sociological functions of defining and providing outlets for cultural taboos, as individuals they are generally treated with am-
bivalence and are not well integrated into normal, everyday
societal roles and functions.

Fisher and Fisher (1981) recently completed a study of 43
professional American comedians who were compared with a
control group of actors. A personality profile of both groups
was constructed on the basis of extensive interviews and
projective psychological testing. Among the more salient findings were that professional comedians struggle with self-
concept issues of smallness and inferiority and are highly pre-
occupied with moral issues of good versus evil. The majority
of the comic sample had been forced to adopt adult-like re-
sponsibilities as children and, as adults, came to view their comic
roles as endowed with priest-like or physician-like functions.
But on the matter of the overall mental health and adjustment
of professional comics, Fisher and Fisher concluded that their
sample showed no unusual amount or quality of personality
disturbance or maladjustment compared to the population as a
whole. Noting that this conclusion was at odds with those of a
previous study (Janus, 1975), as well as popular notions generated in the mass media, Fisher and Fisher assert that they were
"struck with the resilience and psychological toughness of comedians" (p. 10). In a companion study which identified comedians within a college sample, the authors found their amateur
humorists to possess many personality traits associated with
high achievement and healthy adjustment.

Turning to the field of psychopathology, one finds several
clincial groups which show excessive laughter and a heightened

sense of humor. Manic states are characterized by frequent laughter, giggling, and extreme emotional elation generally. "Hysterical laughter" is a common phrase that refers to severe, out-of-control laughter that may proceed to a degree of pain or exhaustion. A particularly vivid example was an outbreak of a "laughing syndrome" that occurred among Central African tribes between 1962 and 1964 (Lambo, 1965). It affected nearly a thousand persons and was diagnosed as hysterical because no organic source could be isolated and because it spread in epidemic proportions but in a highly selective fashion: it began among adolescent females of certain tribes who were attending Christian schools. It spread to the girls' mothers and other female relatives but not to the girls' fathers—in fact, very few males were affected at all. The laughter in question was quite severe; victims would laugh to the point of total exhaustion, and the motor agitation of many was so severe that physical restraints had to be used. Unfortunately, the psychodynamics of the epidemic and the peculiar sociology of its spread have never been fully understood.

Finally there is the inappropriate laughter of the schizophrenics: in the subtype termed hebephrenia (recently deleted as a distinct entity from DSM-III) child-like, silly laughter has been a cardinal distinguishing feature. The inappropriate laughter of other schizophrenics can be distinguished from that of the manic and hysteric by its lower frequency, mild intensity, and primary association with cognitive deficits. Given the schizophrenic's distorted reality testing and thought processes, mundane environmental events acquire incongruous properties. When such incongruities are resolved, the yield is laughter; when they are not, confusion, paranoia, and other symptoms of psychotic pain emerge.

There are also psychopathological groups characterized by a diminished or absent sense of humor. Severe depression dampens or extinguishes the sense of humor. Nussbaum and Michaux (1963) proposed laughter and joking behavior as a useful measure of tracking the course of a depressive episode. Obsessive-compulsives, with their desperate needs and efforts to control and order all facets of their lives, show a diminished sense of humor. Finally, paranoid states also result in a diminished sense of humor; maintaining cognitive vigilance to identify sources of danger precludes the playful frame of mind necessary to enjoy humor.

To summarize, it appears that the relationship between humor and psychological adjustment is no different than the relationship between many other personality traits (e.g., achievement, dependency) and healthy, adaptive functioning: both an exaggerated sense of humor and a poor sense of humor are undesirable signs indicating psychological difficulties.

Chapter 3

Humor and Insight Processes

      The cultivation and expansion of inner experience is a prominent strategy in many systems of psychotherapy. This is usually referred to as "insight" and its specific meaning varies: in psychoanalytic psychotherapies it is making the unconscious conscious; in client-centered therapy it refers to moving toward a more self-enhancing way of perceiving oneself; in rational-emotive therapy it is understanding the irrational assumptions mediating one's behavior. Rosen and Proctor (1981) would classify insight as an "instrumental" outcome of psychotherapy: it is presumed to lead to other "ultimate outcomes" (e.g., increased self-control of behavior) without the therapist's further intervention. The value of insight in promoting such ultimate outcomes has been questioned (e.g., Hobbs, 1962); nevertheless, most psychotherapies—including behavioral approaches—seek to instill in the client a new or expanded awareness of the problems that brought the person to therapy.

      Allport (1961) first demonstrated a kinship between insight and humor. In a study in which subjects rated each other on a large number of personality traits, he reported a correlation of + .88 between ratings of insight and humor. He concluded that in essence they reflect a single phenomenon—man's capacity for self-objectification, the ability to construe oneself as both subject and object.

Fundamentally, humor enjoyment entails mastering a problem that requires an insight solution. Certain social contexts and play signals may prime the participants for amusement, but not all communications under these conditions will elicit laughter. A comment with unexpected allusions or dual meanings will evoke mirth only when its receivers can quickly reason to and vacillate among the various meanings and incongruous juxtapositions. The mental effort spent in achieving such insight is more than half the fun of being there. Memory plays a larger role than reasoning the second time a joke is heard; hence its mirth value drops precipitiously.

Humor has long served as an insight vehicle in political satires and cartoons which seek to change or shape attitudes and beliefs. Many psychotherapists have discovered that humor can serve similar purposes as an intervention tactic during the psychotherapy hour.

Client humor

A number of psychotherapists have found therapeutic benefits in requesting that a client report a favorite joke (Grotjahn, 1949; Zwirling, 1955; Grossman, 1970 & 1977). The technique is an extension of the Freudian hypothesis that unconscious material finds relatively safe expression in tendentious humor. Like the "earliest recollection" method developed by Alfred Adler, a favored joke is presumed to be endowed with psychodynamic significance.

Stronger parallels can be drawn between the favorite joke technique and the classical psychoanalytic method of dream interpretation. Freud published *The Interpretation of Dreams* in 1899; *Jokes and Their Relation to the Unconscious* appeared in 1905 and is replete with Freud's dream terminology (e.g., "jokework"). What are now referred to as the incongruity structures of humor were first labeled by Freud as "condensation" and "displacement" after the two grammatical components of dream language. According to Strachey, Freud's initial interest in the psychoanalysis of humor was sparked by humor embedded within the fabric of dreams reported to him. Having characterized the dream as "the royal road to the unconscious," he apparently viewed the joke as a negotiable alternate route.

There are many similarities between humor and dreams. The illogical, surrealistic, barely coherent imagery and thematic twists of the dream are severe renditions of the incongruity that is basic to humor. In both experiences the individual's attention is drawn away from taboo topics whose presence is thus veiled or set in the background. An often-overlooked feature shared by dreams and jokes is that both are easily forgotten (Grotjahn, 1956). Another parallel is in the way both are unraveled and in the emotional responses which their resolutions elicit. In the case of a joke, emotional arousal is created by both cognitive dissonance (structure) and taboo themes (content). If the play signal is accepted by the receiver, the timing and social context are correct, and the taboo theme is not too threatening, the arousal cascades suddenly into the pleasurable physiological release valve of laughter. If the play signal is refused or other contextual conditions are not met, the same joke yields uneasiness, perplexity, or a hostile response. Dream solution follows a comparable if slower-paced, less intense course. The client who ultimately accepts the "punchline" of the dream may experience an exhilarating (perhaps confused) sense of wonder and awe; the client who resists may experience anxiety, irritation, or may respond defensively.

The following vignette from Zwirling (1955) illustrates the revelation potential of a person's favorite joke:

> A 29-year-old married woman sought therapy for rather vague complaints of sexual frigidity, hostility toward her husband which was reaching a critical point, and an inability to establish a satisfactory relationship with her daughter. She was characterized by an interviewer as "the most overtly masochistic person I have ever seen in this clinic" . . . the older of two daughters, she described her father as a man of puritanical ideals and harsh discipline who expected artistic or professional careers for his daughters. She had almost nothing to say about her mother except that she was devoted to the children and hard-working. The patient readily supplied a favorite joke:
>
> "I have always had to laugh at the one in which a man asked, 'Who was the lady I saw you with last night?' and he answers, 'That was no lady, that was my wife!' "
>
> When the patient had told the joke, the therapist asked "What then happens to a woman when she becomes a wife?" The

patient, always readily brought to tears, began to cry and for the first time spoke with feeling about her mother. (p. 110)

Little psychodynamic sophistication is required to perceive the woman's expression of her personal conflicts through the joke. Additional evidence of the joke's significance lies in her introductory statement "I have always had to laugh." As the vast majority of jokes lose their amusement properties with repetition, "always" having to laugh at this joke suggests that, for this woman, something about it had not been solved.

Proponents of favorite joke interpretation do not contend that the insights it provides to the therapist cannot be achieved by other means. Rather, its value purportedly lies in the light, playful means through which anxiety-provoking conflicts can be surfaced. Grossman (1970) has written that joke-telling is an interaction that a novice client has repeatedly experienced outside of therapy and thus it is not as ominous as reporting one's dreams. This familiarity benefit may be overstated; particularly in a first session, a troubled individual is likely to be taken aback by a therapist who requests a sample of levity. Furthermore, it is doubtful whether a client can experience telling a joke upon request to a psychotherapist in the same vein as the spontaneous "I heard a good one the other day" among friends at a cocktail party. Dream reporting, in fact, may be much more in line with the client's expectations of therapy than telling jokes.

Favorite jokes have other limitations. Zwirling cautions that a joke may be favored by a client because of interpersonal rather than intrapersonal factors. For example, it may be a joke which the client had told numerous times with great success among different audiences. Thus, the favorite joke may be an often-reinforced verbal behavior instead of a voice from the person's unconscious. Another problem is that research has shown that subjects give lower humor ratings to jokes that touch upon personal conflict areas (Levine & Redlich, 1955). Such conflict areas are unlikely to emerge through the favorite joke technique.

Spontaneous client humor must be viewed in an entirely different light. Heuscher (1980) provides an example from a man who used humor to "break the ice" for a discussion of transference feelings:

In another instance, an exceedingly bright and anxious young patient was first able to express his ambivalent feelings toward the therapist by asking him whether he had personalized license plates. When the psychiatrist looked puzzled, the patient remarked casually, "I saw your car in front of your office and wondered whether the BBS on the license plate stood for Big Bull-Shitter!" (p. 1547)

Through humor this client expresses his feelings obliquely and awaits a laugh or smile from the therapist that this new territory is safe to explore. The client may decommit safely from his exploration by saying "I was only joking," if the therapist takes offense. There are other risks inherent to such negotiations. If the therapist reacts with too much amusement, the client may be inclined to pursue more reinforcement by generating more jokes. In such cases the signficance of the joke content pales in comparison to the frequency of joke telling. Joking can be a defensive behavior; as Reik (1949) observed, humor can hide problems as well as reveal them. This danger is particularly acute when treating professional (and nonprofessional) comedians (Ansell, Mindess, et al., 1981). Therapist amusement may also be interpreted by the client as an implicit approval by the therapist of the personal taboo being voiced (Fenichel, 1945).

When the therapist is not amused or inhibits the temptation to smile, other problems may emerge. The therapist risks being perceived as distant and aloof. Worse still is the risk of the client feeling humiliated—particularly if the therapist had initially requested it as a "favorite joke." When the client's humor is spontaneous, it must be viewed as a question about the therapy in general: is this a relationship that mirrors the real world? Or is it something different?

Content interpretation of client humor thus has special pitfalls not shared by dreams and other kinds of therapy material. If the therapist is able to seize the moment, as Zwirling did in the "That was no lady" vignette, there can be client movement. Zwirling's question evolves from the joke; in doing so it conveys empathic recognition of the joke's anchorage in the woman's problems and invites exploration of those problems using the joke as a launching pad. One must assume from the beauty, decisiveness, and outcome of the intervention that Zwirling was cognizant of the client's dynamics before the joke was told. In other instances when there is no such foreknowledge nor an established therapeutic alliance, the hazards of interpreting the content of a client's humor may outweigh its benefits.

Therapist humor

Psychoanalysis and related therapies place a premium upon interpretation as an intervention strategy. As the client talks, the therapist draws inferences as to unconscious anxieties, motivations, and conflicts underlying the client's problems. When evidence mounts sufficiently in support of a particular inference, the therapist offers it to the client as a new perspective upon the client's ongoing experience. If the therapist is skillful in empathically tracking the client and in the timing and wording of the interpretation, the client will accept it and re-evaluate the problems at hand in light of this new information. New insights clash with old perceptions, modifying both; the therapist encourages the client to apply what the client has learned to other aspects of experience. Ultimately the client accomplishes an overhaul of internal psychology; self-control of behavior expands as these new insights color conscious reasoning and decision making processes. The symptom(s) which brought the client to therapy are now vestiges of an old, limited way of construing experience and thus become obsolete.

The interpretation process is seldom as easy as it can be made to sound. Defense mechanism and resistance are terms which refer to a client's effort and style to preserve the old ways of looking at things. Hence psychotherapists have experimented with the "bissociation" (Koestler, 1964) of serious interpretations paired with absurd or incongruous messages in the medium of humor. Humorous interpretations can be insight-facilitating because (1) they render the client an active party in the interpretation process, and (2) the playful context of humor can sometimes circumvent a client's resistance to change.

Client as active participant. "Getting" a good joke and "achieving" new insight into one's behavior have much in common. In both cases success depends only partially upon the person delivering the message; the recipient must actively grapple with cognitive dissonance before resolving it. Interestingly, Greenson (1967) and Weiner (1975) have recommended that interpretations be made with precision timing and economy of words—the same technical requirements of effective humor.

A further connection can be found in the repeated observation of laughter as a client's first response to an effective but nonhumorous interpretation (Freud, 1905; Grotjahn, 1949;

Fromm-Reichmann, 1950; Ferreira, 1959; Schimel, 1978). Ventis (1980), a behavior therapist, suggested that laughter signals a change in a person's cognitive construction of a feared or angering situation. From my experience (Kuhlman, 1982), a married man in his early 20s was once referred to me for systematic desensitization treatment for test anxiety specific to his business courses in college. There had been no evidence that his "blanking out" on the tests was maintained by or related to any deep-seated problem. However, during the hierarchy construction phase of the procedure, problems with his wife surfaced. With an apprehensive seriousness (being a novice and deviating from my supervisor's theoretical orientation) I ventured an interpretation that he was getting back at his wife by failing these courses. The man burst into a boisterous laughter (his most emotionally expressive moment throughout the entire course of therapy)—and then protested that I was wrong and that we return to the desensitization task. The subsequent session he returned to say that he had given my idea some thought and had found a "kernel of truth." While remaining tight-lipped about his marital difficulties and insisting that desensitization continue, he subsequently took his missed exams on his own initiative and passed them easily the first time—long before formal desensitization had begun. By the end of treatment he had passed all four course exams he had missed—and had separated from his wife.

It would be an oversight to view this client's laughter as simply a "nervous" discharge of anxiety related to a painful topic. From a Piagetian point of view, one can infer that the client had a dawning awareness of the relationship between his marriage and test-taking problems and my interpretation provided a "day of reckoning." He was forced to choose whether to accommodate to this information and rearrange his internal construction of the problem ("working through") in its wake— or assimilate it in some fashion that did not challenge his previous schema of isolating the test-taking problem from his marital woes. As noted earlier, laughter and humor production are by-products of a shift from one cognitive stage to another in children and tend to occur when a particular exercise of mastery is new and exhilarating (Levine, 1977). This client's subsequent behavior change suggests that some reorganization of internal reality ("insight") had been achieved which allowed the test-taking problem to be mastered.

Another example in which a client's laughter confirms an interpretation was reported by Jay Haley (1963). Ironically, Haley has been consistently antagonistic toward psychoanalysis and insight approaches to treatment generally. He offered the following vignette as an example of an authoritarian, directive approach to the treatment of a schizophrenic. The schizophrenic and the therapist (who was accompanied by a number of assistants) had been involved in a protracted control struggle in which the schizophrenic had first asserted that he was God. The therapist countered by insisting that he (the therapist) was God. An extended stalemate between them finally ends when the schizophrenic makes, deistically speaking, a tactical mistake:

Patient: Look, you're not supposed to use force against me.

Therapist: I'm boss here.

Patient: You're not supposed to use force—you're not boss here.

Therapist: Who's God?

Patient: I am God.

Therapist: Well, why don't you get up then?

Patient: Well, I'll push them [the assistants] away—tell them to get away.

Therapist: All right boys, get away.

Patient: That was a mistake, I should have pushed them. [The client laughs and everyone laughs.] (Haley, 1963, p. 100)

In this instance behavior change (deferring to the therapist's authority) is followed by an insight ("That was a mistake") sufficient to confirm to all that the person's claims to be God were not psychotic delusions as much as manuevers to maintain control and distance in relating to the therapist. The laughter emerges because the client is faced with the incongruity of claiming to be God but then asking for the therapist's assistance. It serves both as a confirmation to the therapist of the validity of the interventions and as an emotion-laden end to the control struggle that can no longer continue.

When a therapist introduces humor, a play signal(s) must orient the client to a playful perspective. The following example is taken from Grotjahn (1949):

> Once when a patient was unable to see the hostile meaning of his forgetting a name he was told about a friend of the analyst in Germany. It was during the first month of the Hitler regime before everybody woke up to realize the deadly seriousness of

the situation. This group of friends were sitting quite gloomy in a coffee house when a man entered, raised his arm in the newly prescribed salute and said, "Heil! . . . Heil! . . . What was that name?" The result of his very demonstrative forgetting was enormous, and the immediate insight into the aggressive meaning, the depreciation of the Fuehrer, became obvious at once. The meaning of the patient's forgetting became obvious in the analysis, too. (p. 79)

Here an interpretation cast within a joke finds a receptive audience when the conventional modes of interpretation had previously failed. Several dynamisms appear to be working. The client finds it easy to identify with the forgetter in the joke given that the villain is Hitler; thus his own forgetting behavior becomes more palatable. Certainly the content of this joke and others like it which have been recommended (Halpern, 1969; Grossman, 1977) dramatize defense mechanisms more as human nature than human failings. This is important because all interpretations contain a built-in component of criticism, that is, "your way of looking at things is wrong. Try this on for size." When the "wrongness" of the client's ways can be seen as something which the client shares with the rest of humanity (including the therapist who introduces it), it no longer represents a severe narcissistic blow.

Furthermore, split-second mental activity is demanded of the client to move from the depersonalized, "ancient history" reality of the joke to the personalized, present life situation— and to find a link between the two. The joke teaches through the semantic vehicle of metaphor, which has been attributed with several therapeutic functions (Lenrow, 1966; Fine, Pollio, & Simplinson, 1973; Rice, 1974). Metaphor offers an implicit invitation to the client to try out novel ways of looking at behavior. Events are simplified into a schema which permits ready transfer to new situations or old. Metaphor also has evocative properties and involves the client as an active party in the interpretive work. If Grotjahn's interpretation of the forgetting behavior had been worded in common language (e.g., "You are forgetting that name because you are angry at that person"), the client is rendered a passive recipient; he is asked to digest what the therapist has served. There also appears a greater likelihood that the client will swallow whole (or regurgitate) such an interpretation on the therapist's authority alone when the client is not engaged as an active co-therapist.

While proverbial jokes may have these merits, they lack the creativity and empathy of spontaneously humorous interpretations. Consider the following excerpt from Poland (1971):

> The patient was a 43-year-old woman who was in the second year of psychoanalysis with me. At the beginning of one hour the client recounted with great anger how her father had guarded her from seeing books that he considered to be too adult because of their sexual or aggressive content. As a child, whenever she asked to see such a book, he dismissed her with the comment, "No, that's a man's book!"
>
> The patient then went on to speak of her current complaints about her husband, whom she bitterly resented for not being giving enough. She spent the next 20 minutes complaining about men in general. After this she spoke of her dissatisfaction with her analytic work with me, particularly in terms of how little she was getting from me. She went on to say that she had learned a good deal about Karen Horney and was very interested in learning something of Horney's advice on self-analysis.
>
> At this point the patient noticed on my bookcase a copy of Horney's collected papers. She asked me for permission to borrow the book, to which I answered, "No, that's a man's book!"
>
> The patient's initial response was to laugh and to suggest that I said this to try to make her laugh. (p. 635–636)

This articulate, five-word interpretation connects the woman's current problem (dissatisfaction with analysis) with her transference to the analyst as a mixed husband-father figure. Malan (1976) has found that the occurrence of such sophisticated interpretations correlates significantly with positive outcomes in brief psychodynamic psychotherapy. The intervention is best appreciated if one tries to formulate a non-humorous alternative such as "you are simultaneously rejecting me and putting me in a position where I seem to reject you by withholding something from you as your father and husband have done in the past." The sober form is indigestible in length and complexity. The humorous interpretation taxes her attention less, forces her to decipher what meanings the analyst offers, and leaves her considerable choice as to which theme of the communication to follow. Her laughter validates the interpretation and attests to an accommodation-assimilation pivot in which the interpretation vigorously challenges her old "neurotic" perspective. Perhaps it causes too much inner turmoil as the woman backs off from the material at hand and questions the analyst's motives. Note, however, that she did not ask him to explain his humor.

Because Poland's words echoed the woman's own they conveyed a close, empathic contact with her (he calls this "concordant identification"). The outcome of the humor impressed Poland as a signficant insight achievement: "The patient experienced my point as a reinforcement of my alliance with her, using the laughter to move to a position of greater observation from one of simply reliving earlier experiences" (p. 636).

Circumventing resistance. The various segments of the Poland vignette are readily translated into the tactical language of insight-oriented interventions. "No, that's a man's book," is the interpretation; the woman's laughter is a variant of the "aha!" experience that denotes insight. Her subsequent response ("You're just saying that to make me laugh.") is a resistance. In contrast, the standard sequence of insight-oriented therapy is usually conceived as interpretation-resistance-insight. Although it appeared quickly, this woman's resistance was intially bypassed. This resistance-circumventing virtue of humor has been widely acknowledged in the psychoanalytic literature.

Just as defense mechanisms are conceived as warding off undesirable impulses within an individual, resistance refers to an analogous warding off of the therapist within the psychotherapy hour. Specifically, it is the warding off by the client of interpretations, reflections, functional analyses, or advice—any intervention attempts of the therapist. Its origins reside in the assumption that while people seek psychotherapy in order to feel better, they are often less than enthusiastic about the changes required to achieve that goal. They tend to cling to established perspectives and belief systems because they are familiar, "second nature," self-protective, etc. New ways of construing experience which the therapist may provide offer hope—but only after the person is forced to open private skeleton closets. Tarachow (1962) has alluded to another source of resistance. Before a client is able to adopt a new belief system, the client must acknowledge and dismiss the former one as being faulty in some way. Insight thus entails an inherent blow to a client's narcissism or self-esteem; perhaps also a "mourning process" at the loss of old belief systems.

The ability of humor to bypass resistance has been observed by analysts (Grotjahn, 1949, 1970; Rosen, 1963; Rose,

1969; Rosenheim, 1974, 1976) and nonanalysts (Olson, 1976; Ellis, 1977) alike. Rose conceives of humor-laden interpretations as initiating a desensitization process. Rosenheim (1974) suggests that a humor-laden interpretation be tried in an initial interview as a "trial balloon" testing the person's capacity for self-exploration. All of these authors underscore the context of humor as well as its content—a play signal must first be offered to invite a temporary suspension of the otherwise serious connotations of psychotherapy. The play signal will be easily grasped by the client because it takes the same form (facial expression, vocal intonation, body language, etc.) as in "real life" humor interactions. If the client accepts the signal and shifts the ongoing cognitive set to a playful frame of reference, s/he cannot simultaneously maintain a set to ward off the therapist's message. The ultimate effect of humor is thus to provide a sugar coating for a difficult pill.

Consider the following excerpt from Schimel (1978):

Pt.: [*Complaining*]: You always point out the positive aspects of everything.
Psa.: That isn't true.
Pt.: Then what is true?
Psa.: I simply point out the areas you habitually neglect.
Pt.: [*Laughter*] (p. 370)

One can infer that this person was actively resisting some interpretive message of the therapist that had been presented a number of times. Or perhaps the client was resisting the therapist for some other reason (without further context it is unclear whether one or both of these is the case). Schimel's ultimate response bissociates the interpretation of the client's behavior with the client's interpretation of Schimel's behavior. Schimel also negates his own "that isn't true" statement with his punchline, adding another unexpected element to the humorous impact. At the same time he also validates the client's initial complaint about him. Finally, assuming a wry grin or some other play signal preceded Schimel's comments, the client had probably been primed for the laughter that ensued. It is thus difficult, if not impossible, for the client to maintain a resistant attitude with his/her attention span so complexly occupied.

Schimel (1978) on the aftermath of this vignette: "The result is not necessarily insight but an opportunity for insight. The working through, consensual validation, and the repetition necessary for the acquisition of functional insight is still required" (p. 371). As discussed earlier, if the client's laughter is spontaneous and genuine it can be taken as a sign of validation. This validation may only be dimly grasped by the client in the throes of laughter—but it should be firmly grasped by the therapist even as s/he shares in the laughter.

Rose (1969) has recommended the use of a ritualized "one-liner" in response to sexualized transference resistance. This can be a difficult issue when clients (particularly those with borderline character) attach considerable investment to seducing the therapist out of the therapist role. Rose suggests "I bet you say that to all your psychiatrists [sic]" in response to an extraordinary compliment or seductive overture from a client. This quip has a light, nonrejecting quality without avoiding the issue. It also invites the client to stand back from the interchange and explore the therapy-evading functions of the overture.

Killinger (1980) has described a humorous interpretation mode which makes use of visual imagery and physical dramatization to augment insight:

> Another client, David, had developed insight into the stresses he inflicted on himself by being a busybody. He was overinvolved in people's affairs, saw others as too dependent on him, and consequently felt resentful and put-upon, while at the same time anxiously trying to control every situation. As David was coming to this realization, I framed a scene of him as Charles Atlas, standing tall and firmly-planted before us with his huge, bulging, flexed muscles. Perched precariously on top of each bicep sat his worry-wart mom, his long-suffering wife, his condescending boss, and his "free advice" buddy—all pushing and shoving to stay aboard. I got up and pretended to stagger across the room under the weight of it all! We both howled, and David eagerly joined in to add some other things I had forgotten to add to the load. (p. 6)

Killinger's willingness to visualize and behave absurdly augmented the impact of the message and evaporated David's resistance. There was not only laughter to validate the interpretation but also David's adding things to her shoulders that she had neglected. This indicates that considerable "working through" was accomplished. He later reported to Killinger that he regularly called this humorous scene to mind whenever his symptom (bladder problems) recurred. Killinger reports an ultimately positive outcome in which the client's symptom disappeared as his playful, fun-loving, natural talents continued to develop.

Working from an Adlerian perspective, Kadis and Winick (1973) describe the use of popular cartoons as an interpretive device. They see a particular advantage to this visual medium when working with clients "whose continuing verbosity is self-defeating" (p. 108). They are referring to the veteran client involved in an interminable analysis: one who resists the therapist's message by adopting and overdoing the therapist's style of thought. In discussing the problems posed by clients who use this intellectualizing resistance, Kadis and Winick note that "reaching people who are at the point of absolute saturation with words presents a real problem. Yet an appropriate cartoon at the right time may trigger a shock of recognition that leads to therapeutic progress" (p. 110).

> Estelle, a most attractive and intelligent young woman, sought help because she had the normal desire for male companionship but experienced several unpleasant somatic reactions at the mere thought of keeping a date with a man. Gastric difficulties, sweating, flushing, and similar reactions invariably caused her to break the engagement at the last moment. After she had discussed the most recent such episode the therapist showed her a Dean cartoon (see Figure 1) of a very tall man walking on stilts, with a light bulb attached to his behind. A woman standing below the figure looks up at him in awe. Estelle blushed furiously, seemed to shrink, and then said bitterly: "You're right. There's little old helpless no-good me, admiring the man on a pedestal." She reflected that her mother and grandmother had both favored her younger brother, giving him a great deal of attention and admiring all his accomplishments. She felt inferior to him; unable to cope with the overpowering admiration he received, she adopted the same attitude as her mother and grandmother.
>
> At the next session, she said, "What a dope I've been to let this *idée fixe* mess up my life. What makes me act as if all men are godlike when I *know* plenty of them are nobodies? I'm just as silly as that girl in the cartoon to go into a decline when I have a date. It's demeaning and I'm sick of it."
>
> The last time the therapist saw her, about a month later, she related that she had had three dates, and had not experienced flushing, sweating, or diarrhea. Although a little nervous at first, she kept reminding herself that men are only *people*—some special, some not. She didn't feel either unworthy of their friend-

Figure 1

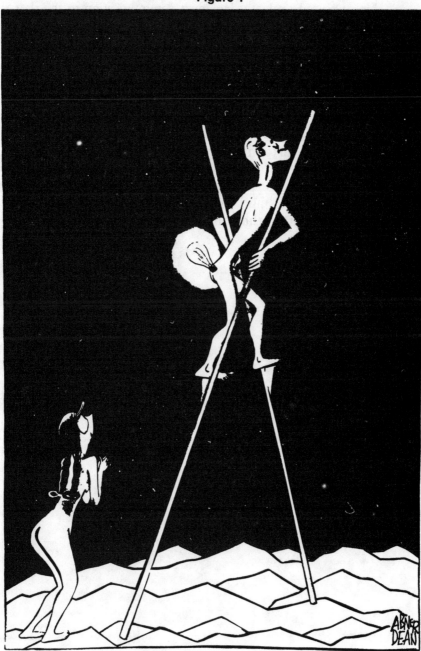

Source: Abner Dean, "The Wonder of You," from *It's a Long Way to Heaven* (New York: Simon & Schuster, 1949).

ship or scared to death. Her next communication to the therapist, six months later, was a one-line note saying, "Men do *not* have light bulbs on their behinds!" (p. 111)

Although these authors interpret through a humorous medium they do not do so with comic intent. They do not allude to play signals given to introduce levity into the situation. Nor do their clients always respond with laughter or mirth; in fact, in two other vignettes which the authors reported, their clients' initial reactions to cartoon interpretations could be described as muted anger.

This points up a crucial consideration: humor-tinged interpretations cannot stand on their own. Their effectiveness must be judged within the context of therapist-client relationship at the moment.

Chapter 4

Humor and Detachment

I was interviewing a 47-year-old divorced, white woman with a spent, tearful facial expression and both wrists heavily bandaged. The night before she had taken an overdose of drugs and had slashed both wrists in a fit of suicidal depression. Her daughter, in another part of the woman's apartment at the time, soon found her and called an ambulance to bring the woman to the emergency room. After sutures and ipecac syrup she spent the night in the emergency room under observation. I was called in the following morning to determine whether her depressed, suicidal condition was severe enough to warrant psychiatric hospitalization.

The woman cried intermittently throughout the interview. She dominated the conversation by reciting a litany of pains, tragedies, and misfortunes, both recent and remote. These included abandonment by her parents and later her husband, a brother murdered in the commission of a crime, a son she hadn't seen in years, a single daughter involved with a married man who left her children with the client for days at a time. The woman was unemployed and subsisting on welfare; she also reported periods of bleak despair which she attributed to the change of life. She had begun to drink heavily the previous few months, and the thought of suicide as her only solution had obsessed her for the previous two weeks.

The woman's self-presentation through her litany was a helpless, passive one of "nobody knows the troubles I've seen." Talking about them with an attentive listener seemed to lift her despondency somewhat, and at the end of 20 minutes, her intermittent crying had ceased. At the end of a long pause she lifted her head from her hands and looked at me for a first extensive period of eye contact. Then she looked down at her bandages and broke into a short, muffled laughter. "You know," she said afterward, "this is like everything else I've done in my life. I can't even kill myself right."

This was a pivotal shift in the course of the interview. It was her first acknowledgement that she had played an active role in the generation of her problems; that these were not simply tragedies that had befallen her. It was a moment of insight wherein she moved away from her prior stance of wallowing in her miseries and was now viewing them as a thoughtful ob-server who was capable of some objectivity.

As her therapist, I could have seized upon the opening that her gallows humor had provided to nudge the insight process further along. A relevant intervention would have been to ask "How is it that you failed at those other things you mentioned?" Indeed, in the context of a regular psychotherapy contact which was some time removed from the suicide attempt, and with a stable, therapist-client relationship established—under these conditions such a question would be the intervention of choice.

But 12 hours removed from a suicide attempt, only mo-ments removed from a tear-stained, depressive soliloquy, and in a relationship only 20 minutes old, intervening in this fashion has many risks. It risks plunging her back into the wherewithal of her suicide attempt too soon. At the time of her self-humor she was much like a swimmer who had been under water too long and had finally fought her way to the surface for a breath of air. Her humor was a momentary mastery of her pain and, under the circumstances, pushing her back down into the water seemed ill-advised.

Thus, I followed my instincts to simply laugh with her and wait for her next move. In not actively intervening I reinforced her momentary sense of mastery and allowed her to take a longer breath of air. She soon returned to her depressive material but did not sink as deeply into it as before; frequent eye contact was maintained and there were no more tears. After a time she inquired about how long she would be required to stay and whether her daughter was still in the emergency room waiting area. I then reunited her with her daughter; they embraced and exchanged intimate words that brought a tearful smile to the client. Before she left I arranged an appointment for her at a local outpatient facility and urged her to use it as a chance to explore whether she had had some control over her difficulties. I was later informed that she had kept the appointment, had been assigned to a time-limited therapy program, had attended all seven of the sessions scheduled for her, and had been terminated as "improved." During two previous contacts with the same clinic at other low points in her life she had come for intake appointments and then no-showed the second one scheduled for her.

In this instance of crisis intervention, the client's choice to absurdly equalize failure at suicide with failure at less momentous tasks (e.g., paying the bills) moved the suicide attempt into the background and out of the limelight. The new focus, her failures, was momentarily mastered with detachment and distance, a process aided by my ability to simply join in her amusement. To promote long-term change, deeper, more intensive work with this woman was indicated. But in the short term, her sense of humor had served her well in deescalating the immediacy and severity of her crisis.

Systematic desensitization

Behavior therapy has traditionally ignored applications of humor in therapy just as psychoanalysis has done. This is not surprising given the early domination of classical and operant conditioning paradigms throughout its infancy. Such schema focus attention upon stimulus, response, and their environmental contingencies, ignoring the "black box" of the mind within which the phenomenon of humor takes place.

In her comprehensive review of theories of humor, Keith-Spiegel (1972) does not identify any theory associated with behaviorism or couched in behaviorist language. Levine (1977) has subsequently suggested that laughter and the sense of amusement be conceived as secondary reinforcers. Insofar as they are initially associated with the new cognitive mastery experiences of the young child, they retain a lifelong association with mastery and success. From this perspective it is reasonable to infer that the semivoluntary, "nervous" laughter which people emit in anxiety-arousing situations represents an attempt to conjure a sense of mastery with respect to a stimulus that is persistently threatening.

The neglect of laughter and humor by behavior therapy seems particularly unfortunate in that the laughter response has much to offer a treatment paradigm such as systematic desensitization. Laughter has a close physiological kinship with fear and anxiety; also, it possesses management and measurement advantages equal to (if not greater than) relaxation which has dominated the "incompatible response" function for 30 years. Virtually everyone can recall a circumstance where a well-conceived, well-timed joke dispelled tension in a previously awkward social situation. And it is ironic that Rose (1969) and other psychoanalysts have used the term *desensitization* in describing how humor can ease the introduction of difficult interpretations.

Reports of humor application in systematic desensitization total only two case studies. Ventis (1973) treated a female college student who requested help at his clinic on the day of a banquet where she was likely to see an anxiety-arousing ex-boyfriend. She feared embarrassment and humiliation at the thought of losing her poise in his presence. As the banquet was hours away, Ventis had no time to train and implement relaxation responses. He and his client developed a five-item desensitization hierarchy and he began the treatment, instructing the woman to relax as best she could. Upon reaching the most anxiety-provoking scene (boyfriend enters the banquet hall with another date), Ventis introduced an unplanned twist—the boyfriend came in with leotards on. The woman broke into a smile; in repeated presentations of the scenes Ventis varied the endings to make them equally absurd. Ultimately, the woman signaled no more anxiety. At the banquet that night she experienced only mild apprehension upon seeing her ex-boyfriend walk in. Moreover, throughout the banquet and the dance that followed it, the woman fantasized one of the humorous scenes from the desensitization session whenever she felt the need for a booster shot of poise.

Ventis chose laughter in this case because of its incompatibility with anxiety. While this notion has inherent appeal, it must be noted that counterconditioning explanations of systematic desensitization have not received empirical support (Wilkins, 1971; Yates, 1975). Furthermore, the woman's coping strategy of conjuring up humorous scenes from her therapy suggests that in order to elicit laughter, the woman first needed to visualize the leotards. In short, a mirth response was not conditioned to the feared stimulus of the boyfriend; rather, the woman distorted the stimulus in fantasy to amuse herself. Explaining the woman's change thus becomes difficult without reference to a "cognitive mediation mechanism" in which the client detaches from the actual feared stimulus and responds to a distorted, fantasized one. Psychoanalysts have coined the term *adaptive regression* for such behavior (see Bellak, Hurvich, & Gediman, 1973). Others (e.g., Singer, 1974) would refer simply to a creative use of visual imagery. Interestingly, the only component of the systematic desensitization paradigm that has been shown to be necessary for treatment success is visual imagining of the feared situation.

A second desensitization case study (Smith, 1973) addressed a more severe and complicated problem. The client was a 22-year-old woman with violent temper outbursts that had become so frequent that her marriage was threatened and she had begun to contemplate suicide. The outbursts were associated with interactions involving her husband and, especially, her child. Smith began traditional systematic desensitization treatment by training the woman in deep muscle relaxation. When the woman could not relax after visualizing anger-provoking scenes for seven sessions, Smith searched for another "competing" response and selected laughter. To evoke this competing response he altered the woman's realistic hierarchy scenes into absurdly exaggerated parodies:

> As you're driving to the supermarket, little Pascal the Rascal begins to get restless. Suddenly he drops from his position on the ceiling and trampolines off the rear seat onto the rear view mirror. From this precarious position, he amuses himself by flashing obscene hand gestures at shocked pedestrians. As you begin to turn into the supermarket parking lot, Pascal alights from his perch and lands with both feet on the accelerator. As the car careens through the parking lot, you hear Pascal observe:

"Hmm . . . 25–80 in 2 sec . . . not bad." But right now your main concern is the two elderly and matronly women that you're bearing down upon. You can see them very clearly, limping toward the door of the supermarket clutching their little bargain coupons. One, who is clutching a prayer book in her other hand, turns and, upon seeing your car approaching at 70 mph, utters a string of profanities, throws her coupons into the air, and lays a strip of Neolite as she springs out of the way and does a swan dive into a nearby open manhole. The other, moving equally as fast, nimbly eludes your car and takes refuge in a nearby shopping cart, which picks up speed as it rolls downhill across the parking lot with Robert Ironside in hot pursuit. (p. 577–578)

With the visualization scenes altered this way, the woman reacted immediately with amusement and laughter; Smith was able to take the client through all the scenes in two hierarchies (one for her husband and one for her child) within one therapy session. Marked improvement was observed and reported after three sessions. In addition to being anger-free during the desensitization trials, real life angry outbursts decreased in frequency and severity. Relatives and friends began to compliment the woman for her "better temper." The woman began to cooperate productively in implementing a behavior modification program for her son and ultimately acquired better control over Pascal the Rascal. Smith also reported significant decreases in heart rate, galvanic skin response, and several MMPI scales (psychasthenia, psychopathic deviate, and paranoia) from pre-therapy to post-therapy measurements.

In light of this dramatic and wide-ranging success, Smith was hesitant to defend the counterconditioning hypothesis he had started with: "Not only did the humorous content of the hierarchy items prevent anger from being aroused, but it also, according to her reports, allowed the patient to view the anger-eliciting situations from a new perspective" (p. 580).

Paradoxical intention

A humorous perspective also serves as a cornerstone of Viktor Frankl's (1967) technique of paradoxical intention. Frankl is best known for his World War II concentration camp experiences; his survival strategy there led him to the development of an existential psychotherapy built upon such concepts as the search for *logos* (meaning) and the fulfillment of *noögenic* (spiritual) needs. Nevertheless, his formulations of common clinical problems have a decided cognitive-behavioral quality. Phobias, for example, are viewed as feedback loops of anticipatory anxiety which crystallize into reflex behavior patterns, irrespective of their origins. The individual's self-statements and excessive intentions to master the feared situation are the fuels that maintain the feedback loops. This mental activity unwittingly assigns the phobic object more power and increases its aversive properties. The individual senses additional fear and accelerates the self-statements and determination to overcome the fear which, in turn, fuels more fear, etc. In a similar vein, obsessions are conceived as self-escalating attempts to fight off unwanted ideas (Frankl, 1968). The energy expended in this "wrong activity" augments the unwantedness of the obsessional material and increases the individual's preoccupation with fighting it.

In paradoxical intention the therapist prescribes the symptom in a massive dose: the client is instructed to intend what s/he fears or to surrender to what s/he has been fighting. The phobic who avoids bridges for fear of a heart attack is instructed to have a heart attack while crossing a bridge. A woman who complained of being obsessed with the idea of looking at men's genitals improved dramatically when instructed to do just that (Kaczanowski, 1967). Success by these methods is understood to remove excess attention and replace it with an attitude of detachment: "taking the wind out of the sails of the neurosis" is a metaphor Frankl repeatedly uses to describe the process.

Paradoxical intention has many apparent similarities with behavioral methods such as flooding and implosion; also with the symptom prescription techniques of Milton Erickson and Jay Haley. Paradoxical intention is best distinguished from these other methods in its explicit emphasis upon a humorous atmosphere as part of the change process:

> The stuttering problem of 17-year-old Horst S. began four years previously during a recitation in class. His schoolmates laughed at him, and their derision became for him a very traumatic experience indeed. Subsequently, his speech difficulty occurred with increasing frequency. Finally he refused to attempt oral recitation altogether. A year before he was treated by a psychiatrist . . . but there were no beneficial results. Dr. E. explained to the patient how the mechanism of anticipatory anx-

iety was involved in the pathogenesis of the trouble, and pointed out the false attitude he had adopted toward it. Though the patient was very pessimistic, Dr. E. succeeded in getting him to say to himself, whenever the stuttering anxiety gripped him: "Oh, I'm afraid that I'll stutter on a 'b' or a 'p!' Well today I think I'll stutter through the whole alphabet for a change!" At first Horst merely laughed at the instructions, but later discovered that this laughter was the heart of the matter . . . though he could not bring himself to actually try paradoxical intention until after the fifth interview, he finally succeeded and after only two more psychotherapeutic sessions was able to resume classroom recitation free of any speech difficulty. (Frankl, 1968, p. 231–232)

There are several paradoxes of intention displayed in the above case. What could seem more incongruous to the client than to have his therapist prescribe increased stuttering to alleviate his intention not to stutter? A steeper paradox is that the therapist seems to be prescribing more suffering under the auspices of being helpful, supportive, and working toward alleviating that suffering. Finally (and increasingly as the client returns for the second, third, fourth, and fifth sessions), there is the realization that the client must agree with the therapist to justify his trust in the treatment—or to minimize the folly of not trusting the therapist and yet returning to see him for five sessions. Tension builds for the client as he is steeped in these multiple layers of cognitive dissonance. The therapist suggests an outlet or resolution for that tension with a play signal: his own humorous attitude. Frankl has variously described the therapeutic effect of paradoxical intention as "distancing" the symptom, "objectivizing" the neurosis, achieving an "existential reorientation" to the problem. If logotherapy is generally conceived as the search for valid meanings in life, paradoxical intention serves the function of detaching the client from invalid, absurd meanings.

In the following example from Gerz (1962), a first session encounter, the psychotherapist is more assertive in cajoling the client toward laughter:

A. S., age 30, mother of four children, was referred to me by her family physician because of the following symptoms: severe panic and anxiety, fear of heart attack, of smothering and strangling. "I cannot swallow. My throat is paralyzed. I have a pressure in my head. I am scared of dying of a heart attack." She complained of dizziness, headaches, and feelings "like taking off

or floating." Also of tingling around her mouth, numbness,
heart pounding, and of "the strangest feelings come over me."
While in my office during her first visit, she was so overwhelmed
by her fear of sudden death that she grabbed my hands, trem-
bled all over, and exclaimed, "Doctor, I must stay with you! I
cannot leave your office! With you I am safe. Check my pulse.
Listen to my heart." In fact, the patient absolutely refused to
leave my office. In this situation, it would not have helped to
explain paradoxical intention because her anxiety was so intense
that she was not able to listen. Her husband was called into the
office and I instructed them to "go downtown and pick out a nice
coffin" for the patient. I asked the husband how much he wanted
to spend on the coffin, and turning to the shocked patient, I said,
"What color silk would you like to have in the coffin—pink or
green?" The husband sensed my intentions. I continued, saying
to the patient, "Go ahead and try as hard as you can to die
instantly from a heart attack" which elicited a smile from her and
the remark, "Doctor, you are teasing." Then, along with her
husband and myself, she was able to join in the laughter . . .

And as she left the office she was instructed not to forget
to "die at least three times a day of a heart attack." (p. 381)

Here Gerz adds satirical exaggeration to paradoxical intention.
This combination, particularly in an initial contact, runs the
risk of alienating the client or being interpreted as ridicule and
rejection. In this instance, the husband's presence and acceptance of the play signal appear crucial; assuming a good marital
relationship exists, the woman is not likely to interpret his
laughter as ridicule. While the therapist is the source of the
humor, the husband's presence and tacit support of the therapist's approach is probably the play signal which the client
accepts.

Frankl has always conceived of paradoxical intention as a
generalist technique rather than a sole province of logotherapy.
In fact, its application has become increasingly eclectic: Haley
(1978) has discussed the method in detail and Shelton and
Ackerman (1973) included paradoxical intention among a col-
lection of behaviorally-oriented therapeutic homework exercises. Paradoxical intention does have drawbacks, most notably
in clients' initial reactions to it. In their published case studies,
Frankl and his followers regularly report that their clients resist
paradoxical intention initially. These case histories are typically
brief, move quickly to the "cure," and do not explain how the
initial resistance is worked through. As most persons seek to

understand their symptoms when seeking relief from them, creating a receptive attitude for a nonsensical technique is an important key to its success. To illustrate, I once treated a 40-year-old woman with a 10-year history of agoraphobia. She had previously been treated by a psychoanalyst (three years) and a behavior therapist (two years). Both therapies had taught her respect for the scientific method despite the fact that she had relapsed at the end of both. When paradoxical intention was first presented to her as an anxiety management technique for use when driving alone, her initial response was "you're joking;" then she became indignant. Providing her with Frankl's rationale for its success did little good; allowing her to read Gerz' (1962) article on his multiple successes with paradoxical intention and discussing the technique with her husband finally melted her resistance to the degree that she was agreeable to trying it. She gradually became proficient, even creative at using paradoxical intention by herself: instead of simply intending a panic attack while driving, she developed her own humorous elaborations (e.g., wishing that the traffic lights would stay red longer). Nevertheless, after practicing it for more than a year she complained it was only helpful when she was at the mild and modest levels of anxiety; never at high levels. As it had been established that all of her anxiety attacks came upon her gradually, I asked her why she never applied paradoxical intention at the early stages of her major attacks. Her explanation was that these attacks were "too serious." Eventually, I inferred that paradoxical intention, to her, was a good, quick mental trick for small problems. But her major anxiety attacks were "not a laughing matter," and the lack of credibility to the technique was never overcome despite her repeated "small" successes with it.

Lamb (1980) reported a novel solution to the credibility problem. She was treating a female college student who reported symptoms of hyperventilation and fainting at the mildest of anxiety-provoking situations. The woman was a student in Lamb's class and was worried that she would pass out, cause a commotion, and fail any examinations unless she was administered the exam on an individual basis. When Lamb suggested paradoxical intention to the woman she was immediately resistant. Lamb then disclosed to the woman that she herself suffered from a seizure disorder and was a far better passer-outer than the student would ever be. She humorously exaggerated the details of her three most recent seizures and issued a challenge to the student: if the woman could pass out better than Lamb, and cause a greater commotion in the classroom, she would receive an A on the test. The student accepted the play signal. During the exam the student began to hyperventilate twice—each time Lamb mimed that this was neither good enough nor caused enough commotion. The student laughed, ultimately completed the exam and the course, and later reported that since the test she had been unable to pass out in any situation. She had taken a humorous attitude toward her fainting and "hyperventilating like a dog on an August afternoon." Lamb proposed that her self-disclosure and modeling self-humor for the client made paradoxical intention more acceptable to the client and thus set the stage for symptom removal.

The humorist as self-actualizer

Humor in treatments like systematic desensitization and paradoxical intention promotes a client's emotional detachment from a focused symptom or problem. For some humanistic psychotherapists, however, humor is a goal rather than a method. In writing about their work these therapists discuss cultivating within their clients a generalized sense of humor toward life experience. The "humorist" is an embodiment of self-actualization, the sense of humor part of a lifelong coping style. This is not a brand of critical humor that disparages the humorist or others, nor one that makes light of the darker side of human existence. Rather, it is a generalized ability to see the tragic and comic views of life as opposite sides of a coin that is perpetually spinning. As Gordon Allport (1950) wrote, "the neurotic who learns to laugh at himself may be on the way to self-management, perhaps to cure" (p. 280).

In describing his Natural High Therapy (NHT), Walter O'Connell (1981a) characterizes humor as "the royal road toward self-actualization" (p. 561). While endorsing Viktor Frankl's notion of the maturity in humor, he questions Frankl's "inherent belief that one simply puts on humor as he does a new pair of gloves" (O'Connell, 1972, p. 166). O'Connell sees the humor of paradoxical intention as forced and artificial; therapeutic humor is more like donning a body stocking than wearing a glove.

NHT is a mixture of concepts and methods found in the work of Ellis, Jung, Moreno, and particularly Alfred Adler. The twin therapeutic goals of self-esteem and social interest are seen as the only realms of experience entirely under an individual's control. Symptoms and emotional disturbance do not result from pathological processes: they emerge as predictable outgrowths of a person's unique personality constrictions and frustrations from one's life history and style of life. NHT encourages the individual to accept full responsibility for problems without blaming either oneself (depression), others (paranoia), or life situations (sociopathy).

Cognitive mediators, such as "hidden demandments" and "negative nonsense," underlie most symptoms and block the pursuit of self-actualization. O'Connell's approach initially calls for empathy which may extend to encouraging such maneuvers. Resistance is seen as a form of cooperation: "The human condition guarantees the presence of chipped edges and incompletion for all humans. Nothing can change this. But tensions, through acceptance, sharing, and humorous responses can become challenges, exciting goals toward actualization" (O'Connell, 1981b, p. 44).

NHT was initially developed in an inpatient setting for the treatment of chronic schizophrenics and drug addicts through a team format. More recently O'Connell has developed "death and transformation labs" to address the problems of the terminally ill. NHT is initially an individual therapy, but the client is expected to graduate quickly into a group. The atmosphere is egalitarian with the therapist modeling actualization through self-disclosure and inviting the client's feedback. Psychodrama, Gestalt exercises, homework, and journal keeping are used (for illustrative case studies, see O'Connell 1979, 1981a).

Humorous interventions by the therapist are not emphasized. Rather, it is the client's sense of humorous transcendence which is fostered as "the essential criterion of the actualization process" (O'Connell, 1981a, p. 564). Humor is an end rather than a means; the humorist is one with sufficient self-esteem to accept personal constrictions. S/he can vacillate continually between the tragic and comic perspective on shortcomings and other irreducible existential paradoxes, achieving meditative space and coping through distance. The humorist stays involved without becoming attached; O'Connell (1975) alludes to the paradox of St. Augustine in describing the actualized style of life: one must live as if what one does is extremely important for the world, but if one died at any moment it would not matter.

The humorist also respects the fact that there are as many different views of reality as there are persons. S/he is willing to share and celebrate mistakes of constriction and neurotic strivings that are universal birthrights of the human condition. S/he seeks and promotes such experiences of universal belongingness.

O'Connell has never discussed specific humor techniques in his writings on therapy process. In his view, humor emerges spontaneously from the client and not at the behest of the therapist. The following is an example of the transformation that occurs in a successful therapy:

> In one case, a World War II veteran who battled traumatic dreams for 37 years, both his mode of perception and quality of dream experience changed dramatically. He started to view the dreams from "above and beyond," no longer huddling in panic on attack boats or pinned down shaking uncontrollably on a beach. In a later dream, he crawled beyond the bloody beach-head to find himself in a shopping center, laughing with glee. He also distanced in time from other old traumata. Bloody comrades became skeletons who could now jest with the patient. (O'Connell, 1981b, p. 43)

Like O'Connell, Harvey Mindess (1971, 1976, 1981) is a well-known proponent of a role for humor in psychotherapy. While he endorses the sense of humor as therapeutic, Mindess also shows restraint in recommending humorous interventions to other psychotherapists. Nevertheless, he views the expansion of a client's sense of humor as an index of expanded freedom and as a sign that the termination phase of therapy has begun.

Mindess views the sense of humor as one operational definition of self-actualization: all life events have tragic and comic sides, and it is up to the individual how to mix and mold these different perspectives. Many of the existential dilemmas which clients bring to therapy are unavoidable or inalterable—one key to mastering them is through ironic detachment.

A humorous attitude by the therapist toward the client's therapy material is not particularly encouraged. Instead the therapist must develop and model a humorous attitude—an attitude of I'm–no–different–from–you–and–here–is–one–

way–I– cope–with–things. Soon the client spontaneously shows a similar sense of self-humor, and the therapist nurtures its development.

Like O'Connell, Mindess views humor more as a goal of therapy than a method. When achieved, the client has increased various adaptive traits: flexibility, spontaneity, unconventionality, shrewdness, playfulness, humility. In an entertaining vignette, Mindess (1976) captures the process as it was experienced by a client outside of a therapy hour:

> It began with a telephone call from a distraught woman whom I had previously known as a student in one of my humor classes. Her marriage was falling apart, she told me, and she was so upset that she felt she had to see me as soon as possible. I gave her an appointment for the next morning. That evening, however, I received another call, this time from her husband. His wife had just attempted suicide, he said, by taking a bottle of pills, and he didn't know what to do. I told him I thought he should try to get her to throw up but, since I am not a medical doctor, I suggested he call the emergency hospital in his neighborhood. This he agreed to do and we agreed as well, if everything was all right, that I would still see his wife the next morning.
>
> Sure enough, at the appointed time she arrived, looking haggard but more or less in her right mind. Then, beginning in a flood of tears and progressing gradually into a combination of consternation and sighs, amusement and laughter, she told me what had happened in the last two days. After 15 years of what she had firmly believed to be a very happy marriage—"a perfect marriage, a union of souls," though because of her own inhibitions they had not enjoyed a satisfying sexual relationship— her husband had confessed to having been unfaithful many times. All through these 15 years, in fact, he had been seeing other women. He had insisted, she said, that he loved her as much as ever, but the revelation of his adulterous affairs was too much for her to bear. In her distress, therefore, she had swallowed the pills as a desperate attempt to force him to prove his love through laying her life on the line. He had responded, of course, as she had hoped, first calling me and then, as I had suggested, the emergency hospital. They had instructed him to make her drink the whites of eggs with plenty of salt, so he had rushed into the kitchen to prepare this emetic. And then, as she told me, she had lain on the bed and waited. And waited. And waited. Finally, growing weaker and dizzier by the moment, she had lurched into the kitchen to discover, in her own words, that

"the stupid bugger didn't know how to separate the yolks from the whites." Needless to say, she had to show him how, so he could save her life, as he had done, and now what remained was a painful, confusing, yet hilarious awareness of the tragicomedy, not just of the previous night but of their entire marital relationship and her previously idealized conception of what it had been. (p. 334–335)

Mindess believes that the biggest obstacle to such masteries is the psychotherapy profession itself. He has referred to psychotherapy as an "inherently ridiculous enterprise" and psychotherapists as "too serious, committed, and fanatic" about their work: "For humor to work, we must be able to take that attitude toward ourselves" (Mindess, 1971). In 1975 he published a poem in the *American Psychologist* entitled "Hail to the Chiefs." The poem lampooned Freud, Jung, Rogers, Perls, and Skinner. While the poem was generally well received, some readers wrote to the editor to complain that it was offensive. Mindess (1976), nevertheless, has continued in his role as the profession's court jester as exemplified by his cartoon (see Figure 2).

Summary

Behavioral, existential, and humanistic approaches to psychotherapy have few areas of agreement. Nevertheless, they converge in showing how humor aids clients in mastering symptoms and emotional problems by distancing or detaching from emotional involvement with them. A general interpretive stance applicable to all the therapeutic humor just described is that clients exert considerably more control over their problems than they initially believe or profess. The therapists do not make such interpretations, however. They prefer to laugh and travel with the client as the latter puts psychological distance between the self and the source of pain.

All would agree that detachment and distancing can be pathological when taken to extremes. The continuous jokester and the clown who never leaves the stage have problems relating meaningfully with anyone except "the Audience." Nevertheless, the healing power of humor, of not taking oneself too seriously, is obvious. It is likely to become a more popular notion in the future given the recent publication of a spate of self-help books (e.g., Peter, 1982) promoting laughter and humor as good medicine.

Figure 2

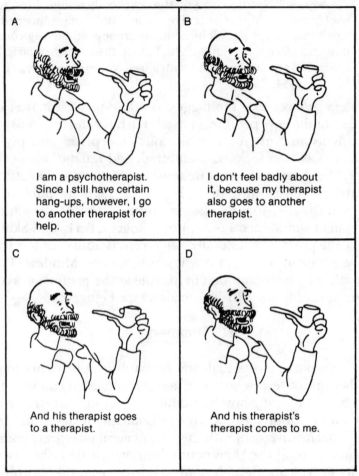

Source: Harvey Mindess, "The Use and Abuse of Humour in Psychotherapy," in *Humour and Laughter: Theory, Research, and Applications,* ed. A. J. Chapman and H. C. Foot (London: John Wiley & Sons, 1976).

Chapter 5

Wit, Sarcasm, Satire, and Ridicule: Therapeutic Functions of Critical Humor

Weiner (1975) has drawn the distinction between strategy and tactics in psychotherapy. Strategy refers to a set of goals or objectives that the therapist is trying to achieve at any given time; tactics refer to the therapist's behaviors or methods that promote the achievement of those goals.

Insight and detachment refer to opposite therapeutic strategies; the various systems of psychotherapy employ both strategies to greater or lesser degrees. Insight strategies steer the client further *into* a problem. They subject the problem to analysis and, hopefully, a resynthesis. Insight strategies encourage the client to view the problem as if it were under a microscope; psychoanalysis, of course, is the most radical proponent of this strategy.

Detachment strategies seek to move the client *away* from a problem, to decrease the client's investment in or preoccupation with it. The client is encouraged to develop a bird's-eye view of the problem; to find a perspective which will diminish its size and impact. Behavior therapy, for example, seeks to detach the client's distressful responses from a particular stimulus, typically by attaching some less problematic responses to it.

Humor functions as a tactic that may serve either strategy. After a humorous interlude is shared and its tension transformed into pleasure, the client or therapist may initiate a backtrack to the particular observation or comment that prompted the moment of merriment. The content themes, how these themes created a moment of cognitive dissonance, and how the dissonance was quickly resolved—any and all of these elements may be subjected to analysis. Or the dyad may implicitly agree to let such an opportunity pass and to allow the humor interlude to fade into the background. The mild elation and momentary intimacy which occur when a sender and receiver converge then colors that which follows it. The therapist who shares in and appreciates a client's humor also validates for the client a sense of mastery and a respite from pain.

As outcomes of humor, insight and detachment (or both simultaneously) can be beneficial at any given moment. For this to occur, however, it must be clear that the amusement was genuine. Forced, nervous, or "canned laughter" signal illusions of insight and mastery. If a therapist's humor fails because s/he has lost the client's empathic track, it is better that the client be able to communicate this with silence, indignation, or some other response indicating that the therapist has "bombed." A mutual trust and respect within the dyad establishes the appropriate context for this to occur.

Some humorous therapists thrive without the normal appearance of such a context. And their humorous interventions seem to assault, belittle, ridicule, or demean the client. Yet they prosper and have waiting lists, and many of them attract students and adherents. And it is most unlikely that their appeal and success hinges solely upon a self-selecting matchup of sadistically inclined therapists with masochistically minded clients.

"Critical humor" is the general term used in this chapter to refer to methods which criticize the client as a tactic to promote change. Cynics and antagonists have often termed such humor "hostile;" any success which such methods enjoy is then attributed to the client's efforts to avoid humiliation by the therapist by doing what the therapist expects. Practitioners of critical humor, however, provide rationales other than sadomasochism or a "corrective emotional experience" to explain why such humor is therapeutically effective. They also adhere to views of the psychotherapy process which are radically different from the more traditional approaches discussed in the previous two chapters.

Rational emotive therapy

While Albert Ellis (1973) once labeled his Rational Emotive Therapy (RET) as humanistic, others have seen it as falling within the scope of cognitive behavior therapy (e.g., Rimm & Masters, 1974). Ellis' tripartite view of emotional disturbance distinguishes between antecedent conditions ("stimuli") and behavioral disturbances ("responses") which are linked by the client's irrational beliefs ("cognitive mediation mechanisms"). RET addresses a specific variety of irrational beliefs: self-statements cast in the form of categorical imperatives (e.g., "I ought . . . ," "I must . . . ," "I should . . ."). Categorical imperatives are associated with excessive degrees of perfectionism, competitiveness, false nobility, self-consciousness and self-absorption, low frustration tolerance, and reduced interpersonal involvement. They reflect and maintain exaggerated narcissism. It is worth noting that as Ellis' RET gained prominence during the 1970s, a corresponding shift was occurring in psychoanalysis away from id and ego psychology to the clinical problems associated with pathological narcissism (Kernberg, 1975) and the emergence of self-psychology (Kohut, 1977). These developments appear to be different systematic efforts to address the casualties of the "me-decade" of the 1960s.

Ellis' approach is more directive and demands a high degree of therapist influence and control. With the goals of "showing people their erroneous demanding and absolutizing," "ideological uprooting," and, waxing more colloquially, "puncture these asinine ideas" (Ellis, 1977), RET pursues an insight strategy. Ultimately, the client is to replace the irrational beliefs with saner, more adaptive self-thoughts. The character of this change is that the client reduces the sense of self-importance with respect to the remainder of the universe.

Categorical imperatives exaggerate the implications of one's behavior. Ellis frequently responds with sarcastic counter-exaggeration to point up the flaws in a client's thinking or presentation:

To this end, I often humorously point out to members of my group, when they confess some stupid act for which they obviously keep condemning themselves, "Of course, no one else in this group ever makes that kind of mistake! Maybe we all had better boycott you for life!" (Ellis, 1977, p. 3)

At one level the message is an encouragement of self-rejection that is canceled by playful overtones. At the group level, public self-martyrdom can be seen as a social tactic designed to move away from the rest of the group and control it by inviting supportive and affiliative responses from the others. Ellis' sarcastic interpretation addresses this second level as well—in humorous exaggeration he argues that the self-martyr be pushed away further, be isolated from any meaningful contact with the rest of the group. This is clearly not what a self-martyr seeks, and the intervention thus encourages a response that will move the client back within the group.

Ellis does not offer apologies nor euphemisms for the put-down, aggressive quality of his humor. He insists that a "hard-headed attack" upon irrational beliefs is required. The play signals of sarcasm include a dry, staccato tone, and anyone who has viewed Ellis *in vivo* or on film can attest to his skill at the sharp, nasal delivery which this medium requires. Furthermore, the amount of exaggeration carried by the word *boycott* is profoundly absurd given the context of an ongoing group working in the intimacy ranges of "therapy." This serves to mitigate the aggressive thrust against the "victim."

Ultimately, in RET, it is desirable for the client to anticipate categorical imperatives before generating them and to laugh at them when they occur. Self-statements become objectified; they are rendered a "thing I do" rather than a part of "I." The client's detachment and distancing from irrational beliefs is a crucial step toward giving them up. Van Den Aardweg (1974), a Dutch psychiatrist, pursues a similar course in his Exaggeration Therapy for homosexuals. He humorously exaggerates self-pity complaints which he theorizes as coming from the "little boy" within a client's personality. The client must learn to make the "little boy" smile and laugh instead of cry—in so doing the "little boy" is transformed from a subject to an object.

Another reason for Ellis' effectiveness with humor is genuine comedic skill:

I therefore continuously interrupt people, in an exaggerated and humorous manner, when they say things like, "She hurts me with her criticism," with, "You mean I hurt me. She, for her own nutty reasons, tries to strike me with verbal arrows. But I foolishly sharpen them up, and stick them in my own breast, and viciously twist. I vastly enjoy that sort of thing—for then I can blame her for my hurt and convince St. Peter that I have sufficient nobility to get into heaven. Of course, he may doubt my nobility and foolishly think that I hurt myself. But that merely would show his bigotry and make me more noble than ever!" (Ellis, 1977, p. 3)

While from the vantage point of therapeutics such a diatribe may arouse controversy, it is difficult not to admire Ellis' creativity. The extended metaphor of "arrows" proceeds to a second extended metaphor of "meeting St. Peter" which then returns to the nobility theme introduced by the first metaphor and reinforces it. The routine thus has an internal thematic consistency, and the theme is clearly grounded in Ellis' theoretical notions about the source of emotional disturbance. The imagery is absurd and its development irrational; but in Ellis' view, one must confront subtle irrational behaviors of the client with dramatic irrational behaviors by the therapist. This is a principle espoused by many varieties of experiential therapies and serves as a rationale for other therapy systems in which critical humor has a tactical role.

This vignette takes on additional meaning if one infers that St. Peter can stand as a symbol for the therapist. The humor can then be viewed as indirectly addressing undertones of the therapist-client relationship in which the client is attempting to elicit the therapist's sympathy. Such an interpretation is apt to meet less resistance in the play context of humor than in the traditional "work language" of psychotherapy. St. Peter is a mediator of Ellis' communication to the client, much as "the Fuehrer" functioned in the vignette of Grotjahn described earlier (p. 47).

Banter and teasing

Sarcastic exaggeration assimilates well into the overall strategy and underlying philosophy of RET. In the majority of psychotherapy systems this is not the case. Critical humor is more typically viewed as anathema to effective treatment; some would even view it as unethical. Nevertheless, adherents of these other systems have discovered advantages to applying sarcasm, wit, satire, and ridicule to episodic or "special circumstance" situations.

Psychoanalysts traditionally place a premium upon the therapist's neutrality and generally take a dim view of responding from a feeling tone elicited by the client. Marie Coleman Nelson (1962) is one psychoanalyst to venture that the treatment of the borderline personality client is an exception to this rule. She proposed the use of "paradigmatic techniques" with such clients. These techniques include the therapist's impersonation of one or more of the client's significant others at various times and asking the client to recommend procedures for the therapist to follow. "Paradigmatic" implies that the therapist must set forth examples of the client's intrapsychic processes or interpersonal relationships. This is in lieu of the client providing such examples (in his/her self-report of life experiences) for the therapist to interpret. Paradigmatic techniques are suited to the borderline personality client with a poorly integrated self-concept and in whom "the ego is composed chiefly of partial introjects and multiple identifications (p. 121)." By dramatizing, acting out, and objectifying the client's psychopathology, the therapist enables the client to respond to a tangible representation of it rather than urge a disorganized, confused individual to introspect into inner chaos. Paradigmatic techniques promote "remedial emotional growth;" eventually the client owns the paradigms that the therapist presents as part of the self, and then the treatment may shift to the more classical, interpretive mode.

Nelson provides a verbatim transcript of a psychotherapy session with a 32-year-old male executive who is described as "almost phobic" about interpretations. Presumably his mother had undergone psychoanalytic treatment when he was a child and had habitually interpreted his behavior to him. He grew up bitter about what he termed her "therapeutic domination" of him, and his transference reaction during treatment was to perceive a therapist's interpretations as attacks. He had unilaterally terminated with three different therapists before entering treatment with Nelson.

The transcript is from the 46th hour of his treatment. The session begins with the topic of the client's recently missed sessions and the fees associated with them. The client initiates a game of psychological chess, seemingly trying to provoke an angry or defensive response from Nelson. He also repeatedly makes interpretations of his own behavior which he attributes to Nelson. She describes her response to this: "I entered into an altercation with the patient; I got tough, spoke sharply, interrupted him, and laid down the law about paying for missed hours. When he suggested that paying for treatment was too much for him, I encouraged him to seek treatment at a clinic. From time to time he accused me of interpreting, which I vigorously denied, arguing—but not interpreting—that *he* was the one who was making interpretations" (p. 128). The client counters by inquiring about a public clinic, its fee structure and location—Nelson matter-of-factly provides him with this information. Ultimately, the client backs off from his threat to leave and then stammers a plea for sympathy to his financial plight.

A 3½-minute silence ensues which Nelson ends by injecting sarcasm:

T1: Have you left for the X clinic already?

P1 [*Laughs*]:   Yeah. I—uh, let's see now. I can't hear a word you're saying. No, uh—[stretches]. This is part of my exhaustion. I almost left for [laughs] sweet dreamland. Um, what am I supposed to say? [Humorously] I can't report this dream, I haven't had it yet.

[Five-minute, 15-second pause.]

P2: Gee, I'm really very tired.

T2 [*Quietly*]:   Well, that was a pretty exhausting exchange we had there. I don't blame you!

P3: Maybe all the work I did—and other things—like I go to the office two nights a week. [Hums gently; 20-second pause]. Why don't *you* talk for a change? Don't you have anything to say?

T3: Why are you rubbing your feet together? Are you masturbating?

P4 [*Laughs*]:   Oh, all right. I thought you had something to say. Why not?

T4: You're not supposed to masturbate in here.

P5: Who said?

T5: I said.

P6 [*Alluding to therapist's standing request that he not remove his jacket* *during sessions*]:   With my jacket on I could. I have my tie on, isn't that good enough? [20-second pause] Well, give me something more interesting to do, like listening to you.

T6:   I'm not here to entertain you.

P7:   Then I'll have to masturbate when I dream. [15-second pause]

T7:   Well, would you like me to read to you?

P8:   You got something interesting?

T8:   Well, I have a pamphlet here on office linoleum. Do you want to hear about office linoleum?

P9   [*Petulantly*]:   No.

T9:   I have a new book here on the *Collected Papers of Frieda Fromm–Reichmann.* [13-second pause]

P10:   Well, whatever you think is interesting. (Nelson, 1962, p. 136–137)

The 40 minutes of the session prior to this excerpt were anger charged and humorless. They ended in a long silence which signaled a stalemate. The therapeutic alliance was in need of repair—Nelson injects a little levity that continues the previous theme (T1). In P1 the client laughs in a momentary bonding but soon resumes the battle with a sarcastic attack on the therapist's orientation. Nelson's silence is a refusal to his invitation. The client reflects on the aftermath of the battle (P2), and Nelson empathizes, implying that she too felt the aftermath (T2). The client backs away from this momentary intimacy in P3 by interpreting his own behavior and then begins a new chess game by asking Nelson for an interpretation. She provides one (T3)—an absurd parody of an interpretation. The client laughs again, outwitted and enjoying it (P4); he acknowledges that he has lost that skirmish but presses on. In T4 Nelson persists in her parody; this time the client resumes the session-long battle, now in the medium of one-upmanship humor (P5–P6). Nelson withdraws (T6) and absorbs a parting shot (P7) which she does not respond to; the client is allowed to claim victory in this skirmish. Nelson sets the client up for a third skirmish (T7); he takes the bait (P8) and is dealt a sarcastic blow (T8). In T9 Nelson seems to recognize that she had hit too hard (P9)—her allusion to a relevant, "psychoanalytic" book seems in part an attempt to make amends through partially decommitting. The session continues in the same vein of bantering and one-upmanship. At the end the client reaffirms his alliance with

Nelson, and his closing comment that the whole session had been absurd is delivered with laughter.

Nelson's discussion of the hour touches on many psychodynamic issues. Of most relevance to her use of humor is the following: "In this highly charged atmosphere I deliberately avoided interpretation of the patient's use of the treatment situation to obtain sadomasochistic gratification, in favor of the more dynamically important nonverbalized message to him: 'We can fight without murdering or leaving each other; I can stand your aggression without throwing you out or killing you off with cold interpretations; I am strong enough to be your father' " (p. 129). The exchange of critical humor thus appears an attempt to shape and define a relationship that the client has not experienced before. As the first 40 minutes of the hour had been open hostility between the two participants, the therapist's shift to the veiled hostility of sarcasm and parody signals an invitation to deescalate the conflict. The client's laughter and humorous counterthrusts validate his alliance with the therapist as the tension level decreases.

Bantering has been cited as a tactic that can facilitate work with obsessive-compulsive individuals who tend to display little or no sense of humor—and a limited capacity for spontaneity, playfulness, and emotional reactivity in general. Salzman (1968) asserts that obsessive-compulsives have a latent sense of humor and light sarcasm is effective with them because it intersects with their tendencies to think only in extremes. Roncoli (1974) suggests that, given such clients' excessive needs for control and order, inducing confusion through the illogic of humor provides a corrective emotional experience within the safe confines of the therapist's office.

> A patient who went to great lengths to improve herself—therapy being one method—spent a good part of a session with me explaining how she was trying to put all "insight" which she was acquiring in therapy into practice. However, in her obsessionally perfectionistic way, she felt she was not doing an adequate enough job. The theme of the interview seemed to be, "See how hard I am working . . . it is not working out the way it should . . . I must be doing something wrong . . . why aren't you helping me more?"
>
> Exasperated by the futility of the patient's efforts to be obsessionally more perfect, I wanted to say to her, "For heaven's

sake—and mine—relax!" Instead, I did an exaggerated impersonation of her behavior, "Please," I said, "be sure you put *everything* we discuss into practice . . . be constantly on the alert that
you don't overlook something." The patient hesitated for a
minute and then laughed. (p. 173)

This form of satirical impersonation—which certainly extended to include the client's vocal tone, facial expressions,
etc.—also issues a paradoxical directive. In this instance the
therapist was emotionally taxed by the client's obsessional behaviors. Hostility and aggression are common responses toward
one who "exasperates," and Roncoli's ridiculing satire has a
sharp edge. Nevertheless, the client's laughter suggests that
she did not perceive it as an attack. Her initial hesitation be-
speaks uncertainty and surprise but does not yield a counterattack or indignation. Furthermore, her amusement serves
as a brief vacation period from the workaholic cognition that
afflicted her.

Harold Greenwald (1967, 1975) is a master of light, satirical impersonation which he refers to as a mirroring technique.
Its goal is to give the client insight as to how s/he appears to the
rest of the world.

> A rather serious career woman found it difficult to talk
> during our sessions, and the less she spoke, the more anxious she
> became. The greater the anxiety, the less she could speak. Trying
> to find the causes of this difficulty I encouraged her to speak
> more about how she talked to her parents; she told me that as a
> young child she often found the only way she could speak to her
> father was if she was under the table in the dining room.
>
> "Why don't you get under the desk?" I asked her.
>
> "Oh, I couldn't do that," she answered with a giggle, "Why
> don't *you* ?" she challenged.
>
> Happily, I perched under my large desk for the rest of the
> session; she spoke with much greater ease. At the next session
> when she hesitated I started to get under the desk again and she
> stopped me, saying "OK, OK, I'll talk just don't go under that
> damn desk again." Then she added thoughtfully, "I guess I've
> been afraid to make a fool of myself by saying something silly or
> stupid. But since you showed me that you don't mind making a
> fool of yourself, why should I?" (Greenwald, 1967, 44–45)

Unlike most other humorous therapists, Greenwald does
not attempt to justify his antics by appealing to a theoretical
rationale: "Fortunately, as I began to be more confident of my

craft I returned to my more normal state of being and discovered ways of making my naturally playful disposition useful to my patients" (Greenwald, 1967, p. 44). Anyone who has witnessed a presentation by Greenwald can attest to his considerable comedic skills; his methods may not fare as well in the hands of a therapist who lacks such skills.

The effects of banter, sarcasm, and satire depend heavily upon the play signal interchange which precedes them and the delivery style that accompanies them. A stable, mutually trusting therapeutic alliance is another important contextual feature; without it banter is risky, if not dangerous. Coleman (1962), a psychoanalyst, has proposed that banter has a place in short-term, goal-oriented therapy—and he reported having successfully trained novice psychotherapists (psychiatric residents) in its use with clients seeking help at a public outpatient clinic. He suggests that bantering is indicated with clients who share the following characteristics: lower socioeconomic status and education, minimal psychological mindedness, and a desire to obtain symptom relief rather than self-understanding. Such clients tend to be well on the road to spontaneous recovery by the time they first come to a clinic and do not expect or comply with an extended period of therapy sessions. They also attempt to aggress against the therapist and to shape the therapeutic relationship through a masochistic maneuver—"absurdly self-pitying and manifestly insincere protestations of abuse of the innocent" (p. 71–72).

> When a patient complains in one way or another, about not being liked or being ugly, the therapist may say, "Who can like you anyway?" Or, "Why did I have to get stuck with you?" Or, "You're the worst patient I ever had." This is said in a friendly tone and tends to have a comforting effect upon the patient. (Coleman, 1962, p. 72)

Another example of such banter by Harvey Mindess (1976) occurred during an initial session:

> For example, a young woman suffering from severe anxiety consulted me. It was the first time she had ever visited a psychotherapist and she told me she had been reluctant to come. She had heard, she said, that therapists not only failed to help many patients but that they frequently harmed them . . .
> What I said was, "Well, you're in luck. I've already destroyed my quota for this week." Her response was rich laughter. (p. 336)

In both of these vignettes the therapists join with the clients' resistances by agreeing with their premises. The "data" they then offer to further support the clients' premises is incongruous with their role as help-givers. The clients undoubtedly expected the therapists to dispute the premises with them while maintaining the sympathetic, help-giving role. The clients' laughter signifies an end to the chess game—and some relief that the therapist refused to be drawn in to play it.

Provocative humor

Bland or flat affect and social isolation are two hallmark symptoms of schizophrenia. Psychotherapy with schizophrenic individuals is taxing and difficult; considerable time and effort is required to achieve the depth of interpersonal contact necessary for the establishment of a therapeutic alliance. It is not uncommon for the therapist to experience emotional burnout, detachment, and social withdrawal in response to the frustrations posed by the schizophrenic client.

Before shifting to their current interest in marital and family therapy, Carl Whitaker and his associates championed the approach of working with schizophrenics by responding with a wide range of bizarre and incongruous behaviors (Whitaker & Malone, 1953; Malone, Whitaker, Warkentin, & Felder, 1961; Whitaker, Felder, Malone, & Warkentin, 1962). They argued that the objective in the early phases of psychotherapy with the schizophrenic should be to provoke or manipulate any expression of affect that the client is capable of. Anger, rage, and confusion are more productive than apathy if the schizophrenic is to form a meaningful therapist-client relationship that is not tied to the client's delusional systems. To this end the therapist must be prepared to revert to traditionally "untherapeutic" responses including publicly denying an interest in helping the client, telling dirty jokes, going to sleep during the therapy hour, etc. (Whitaker et al., 1962). From reading the clinical vignettes offered as examples of Whitaker's approach, one might infer that his therapy sessions were filled with laughter and mirth. Nevertheless, Whitaker did not specifically advocate a humorous atmosphere to his irrational psychotherapy, nor did he imply that the therapist should offer play signals that would negate or mollify the therapist's seeming rejection of the client.

Like Whitaker, Frank Farrelly initially developed his Provocative Therapy (PT) for chronic schizophrenics with a similar goal of provoking emotional responsiveness from this hard-to-reach group (Farrelly & Brandsma, 1974; Farrelly & Matthews, 1981). Unlike Whitaker, Farrelly places a premium upon a humorous atmosphere and stresses the importance of gestures, vocal intonations, and other play signals. These accompany and qualify a verbal assault on the client that is often vicious and unremitting. The client is confronted and attacked until s/he laughs: "We need to stress here again that *if their client is not laughing at least some of the time,* then they are not doing provocative therapy" (Farrelly & Brandsma, 1974, p. 99).

T [*Continuing to grimace*]:   It's just you're just such a . . . stumble-bum and inept and . . . ugh! [T finishes by gesturing helplessly and sighing as though saying "words fail me—I can't express how ugh you are!"]

P [*Evenly*]:   All right, I think . . . I think the thing that has been *missing* the most in my life . . . and the reason I'm such a stumble-bum and so . . . ineffective . . .

T [*Flatly interjecting*]:   Yeah.

P   is that I don't, I don't care for myself,

T [*Supportively*]:   Well, I don't blame you.

P [*Continuing uninterruptedly*]:   and I never have.

T [*Supportively*]:   Well, I don't blame ya! . . . That's some—I'm happy to hear you've got *some* judgment.

P [*Pause, nonplussed*]:   Wellll, I . . . as I look back on my child-hood . . .

T [*Wearily*]:   Oh, must we? Oh, go ahead if you must . . .

P [*Gingerly proceeding*]:   . . . there wasn't anything I did . . . that . . . that gave me any reason for . . . for disliking myself intensely.

T [*Flatly*]:   Well, you got it somewhere . . . you've had . . . plenty of reasons since then.

P [*Pause, persuading*]:   But it's because I don't like myself that I do these things.

T [*Remonstrating*]:   No, no, no! It's because you do these things that's why you

P [*Interjecting*]:   No.

T [*Finishing*]:   don't like yourself.

P [*Louder*]:   No.

T [*Overriding her*]:   Oh, you got it all back-asswards.

P [*Even more loudly and firmly*]:   You're wrong!

T [*Matching her tone*]:   What do you mean, I'm wrong?

P [*Attempting to explain*]:   It's 'cause . . .

T [*Pompously; not waiting for her reply*]:   Hell, you're just a patient and I'm a therapist. Now how the hell do you know . . . where do you get off telling me I'm wrong?

P [*Evenly; with assurance*]:   Well, you're not infallible, Mr. Frank Farrelly.

T [*Laughs*]:   Oh, I'm not? And I could be wrong, is that what you mean?

P [*With assured firmness*]:   Yes, you're wrong. You're wrong about me. I'm not as . . . as evil, and not as wicked and not as . . . damnable, and not as . . . as hopeless . . . [Phone rings; P ignoring it, finishing] and not as . . . [Phone rings again; T puts hand on receiver but doesn't lift it, waits for P to finish] . . . inadequate as you . . . contend! [P laughs, nods head abruptly] *There!* (p. 103–104).

PT could be characterized as the Don Rickles school of psychotherapy—and as the stylistic designations in the brackets of the vignette indicate, it is conducted in a theatrical manner. Exaggeration is the syntax of the "four languages" of the provocative therapist: religious moralism, locker-room and street language, professional jargon, and body/kinesthetic expression (Farrelly & Matthews, 1981).

Farrelly is candid about the origins of PT—a session with a woman client in which his pants fly was inadvertently unzipped as he and his client discussed her sexual infidelity toward her husband. He acknowledges that PT fits and reflects his own personality and that the theory of personality change which underlies it was developed after the fact. Ironically, he was strongly influenced by Carl Rogers and took part in the schizophrenia project conducted by Rogers at Mendota Mental Health Institute. While his methods hardly appear client-centered, Farrelly's philosophy of man reflects Rogerian principles. These include the assumptions that clients have more potential and less fragility than psychotherapists usually assume, and that people grow and change in response to a challenge. He deviates from Rogers in his contention that clients will move in a direction opposite to the stance taken by the therapist and in this respect aligns better with Erickson, Haley, Whitaker, and others who advocate paradoxical techniques. As the vignette illustrates, the therapist confronts, provokes, and attacks the client unmercifully until the client defends herself by fighting back. The typical process of PT involves four stages: the client is first astonished or confused by the attacks but soon recognizes their validity (insight). The third stage is resistance, in which the client fights back against the therapist, and the final stage is detachment, in which the client begins to laugh at the "old self." Microcosms of these four stages are evident in the vignette.

The provocative therapist takes a no-holds-barred approach to assault tactics: "In Provocative Therapy, the therapist can 'lie,' deny, rationalize, invent phony 'research' data, 'cry' and think and act 'crazy' " (Farrelly & Matthews, 1981, p. 686). S/he can send contradictory messages, deliberately "misunderstand" the client, or offer wildly distorted psychological explanations for behavior. The strategy behind these tactics is to put the client in an inferior position in order to motivate coping responses. "The provocative therapist would rather offer genuine rejection for a given client behavior than a phony constrained acceptance" (Farrelly & Matthews, 1981, p. 683).

In the medium of printed language, PT is difficult to distinguish from verbal sadism. Farrelly's contention that play signals are always prominent and that "tongue-in-cheek" aspects of the therapist's assault convey acceptance and warmth clash with his labeling of cases (e.g., "Clem Kadiddlehopper," "The Slutty Virgin," "The Malingering Nut," etc.). It is also a strain to infer decommitment in some of the examples of PT interventions that are offered.

P [*Snarling*]: I am going to kick your goddamn teeth down your fucking throat.

T [*Looking levelly at the patient*]: Yeah? And what do you think I am going to be doing while you're kicking my goddamn teeth down my fucking throat?

P [*Taken aback; pauses, muttering sulkily*]: You'll bite my foot off at the ankle.

T [*nodding and smiling*]: You got it, you bitch. (Farrelly & Brandsma, 1974, p. 49–50)

Countering a client's hostility with an equal measure of hostility is obviously not taboo in PT. Nor are apologies offered for it: "Often in therapy, distinction must be made between short-term cruelty with long-term kindness versus short-term kindness and long-term detriment" (Farrelly and Matthews, 1981, p. 683–684). An aspect of PT that qualifies its aggression is the therapist's avoidance of professional dignity and willingness to lose face and even turn the hostility upon the self. In the first PT vignette, Farrelly makes a mockery of himself by exaggerating his therapeutic omnipotence and thus rendering himself defenseless to the client's counterattack. In this light, PT does not always appear to be a one-upmanship competition played on the field of hostile humor.

A crisis model of critical humor

The dangers associated with critical humor are more obvious than its benefits. Yet some therapists have clearly flourished with witticisms and put-downs, and their assertions as to the therapeutic effects of aggressive humor merit close examination.

One frequently encounters the contention that critical humor which is therapeutic attacks the client's behavior but not the client. Ellis (1977), for example, writes "I consider it *verboten*, in the course of therapy, to poke fun at people, even though I frequently ridicule their fatuous and self-sabotaging ideas" (p. 2–3). Farrelly and Brandsma (1974) assert "We ridicule the person's screwball, idiotic ideas and behaviors but not the person himself" (p. 104–105). Such statements sound impressively humane and may clearly represent the intentions of their authors. Yet both Ellis and Farrelly also acknowledge difficulties in operationalizing the distinction between attacking the client's behavior and attacking the client. And if the therapists have difficulty articulating this difference, what of the clients?

An inspection of the language used by therapists in the humorous interventions presented thus far appears relevant. In virtually all of the vignettes presented in the earlier chapters, the therapists' language addresses client behaviors rather than clients. In the examples drawn from the writings of Ellis and Farrelly, the language of the interventions appears directed at the client rather than an isolated aspect of the client's behavior.

Thus the "attack the behavior but not the client" rationale appears to be a specious explanation that is disputed by available data. It is also an oversimplification; it violates the interactional nature of a humor interchange wherein the receiver chooses to accept or reject the sender's invitation to "play." It is reminiscent of the "We are laughing *with* you, not *at* you" rejoinder made to a receiver who responds like a victim to some humor that was off the mark. While "with you" may have been the sender's intent, it cannot erase the receiver's initial experience of feeling assaulted. In fact, such a decommitment message by the sender serves to add insult to injury: after initially feeling victimized, the receiver is then made to feel like a fool.

A more cogent explanation for the therapeutic effects of critical humor evolves from viewing it as a momentary crisis situation (Caplan, 1964). Crisis is created by multiple levels of paradox: first, the incongruity inherent to the humor technique itself and the manner in which this incongruity is quickly resolved. Second, there is the paradox of the therapist in the role of help-giver and pain-reliever who is choosing to mock, satirize, or ridicule the client. Third, is the fact that the client is paying the therapist money for the opportunity to be abused. Finally, there are the therapist's play signals and mode of delivery which qualify or undermine the assault as "not real." Occurring simultaneously, these paradoxes are a dose of ephemeral stress to the client who is momentarily overwhelmed by ambiguity, uncertainty, and cognitive dissonance. However, as in Caplan's concept of crisis generally, they also create an opportunity for significant change and an openness to novel problem-solving strategies. Thus Ellis' client may quickly grasp the irrational imperatives mediating behavior, and Farrelly's client may immediately rise up and counterattack in self-defense.

Crises, however, do not resolve magically; a support system is usually required. The therapist must maintain this role throughout the generation, maintenance, and follow-up of the humor. Critical humor imposes a double bind on the client; it is the converse of the pathogenic one associated with schizophrenic families wherein a manifest communication is warm and supportive but the latent communication is hostile and rejecting. For critical humor to be effective requires that beneath the manifestly critical, even sadistic assault from the therapist, undertones of caring, concern, respect are communicated. In Greenwald's (1975) words:

> Your humor must be based on your liking people and your appreciation of them. Your appreciation of their strengths and

their abilities, when expressed in humor, gives them this un-spoken message: "I know you are suffering right now, but I also know that you have the strength and ability to get away from that suffering, to look at it, to see what you can do with it, and how you can decide to change, how you can master the situation." (p. 115–116)

Chapter 6

Risks and Dangers

Published case studies depicting failures are rare in the psychotherapy literature for obvious reasons. Of the approximately 30 psychotherapists and counselors who have written about humor, all but 1 emphasize it virtues. The only author to write against humor (Lawrence Kubie) cites one failure case—and it is not a failure of his own. This is an unusual phenomenon in the psychotherapy literature. More typically an intervention theory, strategy, or tactic is introduced and a counterreaction from opponents ensues, leading to a scholarly debate or controversy.

That this is not true for humor can be attributed to the fact that its dangers and pitfalls are known to all. We have all experienced the pain of being mocked, teased, ridiculed, or laughed at. The veil covering aggressive intent can be virtually transparent in a circumstance in which the sender-receiver relationship contains no auspices for play. Moreover, the cruelty of hostile humor can be greater than that of a direct insult. For in addition to the aggressive intent there is a violation of the rules and spirit of play: a violation of the freedom, pleasure, bonding, and intimacy that are shared by the participants in moments of true laughter.

Hostile humor also poses its victim response problems greater than those of direct verbal aggression. If the antagonism in the sender-receiver relationship had not been mutually apparent beforehand, the receiver may experience some momentary confusion and doubt before concluding that the play signal was a red herring. The fleeting nature of a humorous interaction is such that anything but an immediate response is socially inept and "loses points" for the victim in the eyes of real (or fantasized) onlookers. If the structure or technique of the sender's hostile humor is clever, the surprised victim will have difficulty responding adequately in kind. One's creative abilities are hampered after taking an unexpected blow.

It must be reemphasized that whether such humor represents antisocial aggression or teasing with decommitment, or well-meaning criticism or a paradoxical display of affection—these various meanings are not defined by the joke's technique or content. "Nice shot, nigger!" said by a black man to his black teammate, after the latter has made an exceptional move and shot to the basket, is a form of high tribute. The same comment made by a white teammate is ambiguous; if made by a white teammate after the black has missed a shot, it represents an invitation to open hostility. The quantity and quality of play signals modulate the amount of sender decommitment from the hostile message; "dry" humor is that in which play signals are subtle or entirely absent. Relationship factors, particularly what had transpired between sender and receiver immediately prior to the "humor," aid the receiver in decoding the degree of the sender's decommitment. Feeling "laughed at" occurs when play signals are not processed accurately by the receiver or previously antagonistic aspects of the sender-receiver relationship mitigate their impact. "Laughed with" experiences accompany easily processed play signals in the context of a positive sender-receiver relationship. There is much gray area in between.

The present chapter focuses upon these gray area dangers of humor. I will assume that the black area dangers—those that arise when therapists abuse their power base in the relationship by acting out aggressive urges beneath the illusion of "therapeutic" humor—are infrequent and readily self-evident. If this assumption is naive, it remains doubtful whether an extended discussion of "black humor" would aid abusers in discontinuing its practice. Consumer complaints to professional regulatory boards represent the best remedy to that problem.

A non-empathic intervention

A comment by a therapist who adopts a humorous attitude toward the client's material is the antithesis of the Rogerian empathic response. When it is salient to and anchored in what the client has expressed immediately beforehand, a humorous intervention is a reflection to the client of the "photographic negative" of the client's experience rather than the "color print." Form and pattern are retained, but the therapist's comic distance obliterates color, shading, and nuances of detail. If the relationship and its proceedings have been predominantly positive, such a breach of empathy may enhance the therapeutic endeavor—if for no other reason, in the way that comic relief enhances the unfolding and resolution of a tragedy. However, if the therapist's tracking is "off," considerable damage may be done. In the following case which I conducted, a first attempt at light sarcasm in the seventh hour of a therapy had unfortunate and unremedied consequences.

John was a tall, handsome, muscular boy of 19; visually he was quite appealing, neatly dressed, and well mannered. His speech was in sharp contrast to his appearance. His voice was soft, meek, and high pitched; its cadence was tentative, halting, and noncommittal. He sought therapy after a verbal altercation with his father that ended with John cutting his wrists in both parents' presence. Later he explained the suicidal gesture as motivated by doubts of whether or not his mother loved him. Two years earlier John had started therapy after a similar conflict in which he had threatened both of his parents with a knife. He had appeared for two sessions and then dropped out with no explanation after efforts by the therapist to get his parents involved were fruitless.

At the time I began working with him, John was extremely sensitive and introverted. He maintained a calm, passive, seemingly angelic demeanor and was constantly vigilant to approval/rejection signals from me. He was also prone to violent, explosive rages when alone—this was a lifelong trait that typically resulted in damage to his home or furniture two or three times a year.

His childhood history was unremarkable except that he had always been a shy, sensitive, wallflower sort of boy. He had been an average student who dropped out of high school when a first factory job came along. At the time I began working with him, he had been laid off for six months; two months into his unemployment the only girlfriend he had ever had broke up with him. Initially he had been severely depressed by this, but he soon got over it after his mother had urged him to become more interested in his religion. He had since become heavily invested in his fundamentalist church, and the only time he ventured out of his home was to attend services, prayer meetings, and related social events. He also read the Bible frequently at home, and religion-related themes colored half of his spontaneous communications early in the therapy. At such times his voice showed better volume and steadiness, and his facial expressions would convey a sense of peace and tranquility.

Aside from church he avoided the outside world, alternately expressing disdain for the sinful ways of most of his peer group and anxiety that they would see him as awkward, incompetent, and unlikable. He was highly self-critical, guilt-ridden, and self-abasing. He wrote the following joke as his favorite on an intake form prior to beginning therapy:

> A man went into a bar and wanted a drink. The bartender said, "If you drink out of this spittoon I'll give you a bottle of whiskey." He started to drink until the bartender said, "OK, you can stop now and take the whiskey." Still the man kept drinking until everything in the spittoon was gone.
>
> The bartender then handed him his bottle. "Here's your whiskey. Why didn't you stop when I told you to?"
>
> The drunk [*sic*] said, "I couldn't. The spit was all in one long string."

This joke was never discussed during therapy, although its self-degradation theme was salient to his psychological condition at the time. The extreme degree of self-abasement reflected in the joke and its disgusting nature were highly incongruous with John's overly-controlled, Bible-quoting demeanor; such an extreme was important to the funniness of the joke to John, in the sense that it provided a certain degree of mastery over his low self-esteem (i.e., "I may be a disgusting person, but I'm not *that* bad.").

The joke also intersected with John's barely bottled-up rage at his father, who had been an alcoholic as long as John could remember. John was his father's favorite and usually was spared his father's drunken wrath. This was regularly heaped upon John's mother and older brother (by one year) when the father returned home from work at night. The abuse was only verbal but intense; John was amazed at how his mother had tolerated it for years and yet continued to wait on his father hand-and-foot. His older brother was skilled at tuning the father out; he would retire to his room or spend the evening on the streets engaging in mildly delinquent behaviors. John felt estranged from the older brother, who was his mother's favorite.

John had always felt insecure of his mother's love and ambivalent about his "accidental" specialness to the father who repeatedly abused her. He never remembered his mother being cold or rejecting toward him, but he had always had a desire to be closer to her. During his homebound unemployment period, John confined himself to helping his mother around the house, providing emotional support to her, and generally trying to make her life easier. She, in turn, had begun confiding to him more than in the past, and they attended church services together for the first time in years. Gradually John began to see himself as his mother's protector and buffer from the rages of his father. On the night of his suicide gesture, however, his mother had joined forces with the father in the middle of the altercation and demanded that John stop defending her and show some respect to his father. It was at this point that John took a knife from the kitchen drawer and ran to the bathroom to cut himself.

I worked with John in therapy for seven individual sessions after his father flatly refused involvement; his mother also refused to be involved except to support John's coming individually. She stated over the phone her belief that John needed to "get out on his own—it's his only hope in a crazy family like this one." From John's subsequent reports, she supported this position in her interactions with him at home. She stopped relying upon him as a surrogate husband but did so without withdrawing her affection for him as a son.

John's acute symptoms (depression and temper outbursts) remitted quickly. In addition to his mother's change of behavior, my availability as an empathic, nonjudgmental, and uninvolved helper was important. He quickly grew comfortable in the client role and by the third session began questioning his mother's role in the family problems in not standing up to the father and not divorcing him. Subsequent to that session, he began retiring to his room to read his Bible when his father would come home from work, and if he heard his parents' voices raised he would say a prayer for them rather than join the fray. He began to attempt a rapprochement with his older brother and made some phone calls to see about earning a driver's license and his G.E.D. (two omissions he was ashamed of) while he was laid off and had time to pursue them. He also began considering enrollment at a technical college to pursue a career as an electrician after earning his G.E.D.

In sessions 4, 5, and 6 he verbalized some disillusionment with both his mother and his father. He also had begun to detach from his church group, venting uncharacteristic verbal anger at his church's leaders and the sordid things he had learned about their private lives. As he began these detachments, his attachment to me became stronger: in session 6 he stated that he didn't respect his parents, didn't respect his church, didn't respect anyone "except you, you've made something of your life." At that time (and later) I viewed this statement as indicating a nonpathological, good role model/father perception of me. Up to that time my stance with him had been predominantly client-centered; I had provided him with very little direction, few instructions, and the one instance in which I had given him a homework assignment he had chosen not to do it because it did not have relevance to him after he had left my office and gone home. He did not make special requests of me, did not inquire about my personal life, and did not make phone contact in between sessions.

One problem area in which I had been structuring and directive concerned his reluctance to become involved with his peer group outside of the home. The not-too-distant rejection by his girlfriend and the subsequent period of immersion solely in family and church matters had rendered him almost phobic about unstructured peer relationships. He wanted to avoid contacting friends he had broken ties with until he was again employed, had a driver's license, and had passed the G.E.D. test. I actively disputed this with him, and he acknowledged that those achievements would not magically remove his self-confidence problems and that continued peer isolation would make it even harder for him.

In session 7 we were discussing various reinvolvement strategies for him. He had called a male friend who had been glad to hear from him, and had left it up to John to decide where they might go out the coming Friday night. It was a light, pleasant atmosphere as he inventoried the various bars and hangouts they might go to. At times he would editorialize humorously about unusual incidents he had witnessed or heard about at specific places. A dance hall type of place occurred to him, and he speculated aloud as to what could happen to him there:

John [*Talking matter-of-factly at first; speech growing progressively more tentative*]:   You know, a lot of neat girls go there. Sometimes they ask the guys to dance! [*Pause*] If I made a fool of myself there, I know I'd want to just jump out the window.

Author [*Lightly*]:   "Well, if you do, put it off until our next session and I'll let you use one of the windows in my building here. It would probably work better here anyway; we're seven stories off the ground.

John [*Brief laughter, breaks eye contact by looking down at the floor. Continues matter-of-factly*]:   Or maybe we could go down to the baseball game if the Reds are playing at home this week . . .

The inventory of social outlets continued, and ultimately a choice was made; I noted that the light atmosphere that preceded my quip had changed slightly, but I did not comment about it. The session ended without any remarkable incidents. John canceled the next session with my secretary and rescheduled for the following week. When he did not appear or call I contacted him to hear that he had overslept, would be in next week, and things were OK. The following week his mother called an hour before his appointment to say that the family situation had gotten worse again and John had elected to go south to stay with an uncle for a couple of weeks. If things worked out there he might look for a job and stay for an extended period. He had left the previous day and would send his check through the mail.

A month later I called John's home to learn how he was faring, and John answered the phone. He had been back two weeks and immediately volunteered that he would get a check to me in the mail soon as he would be going back to work at the factory three days hence. I asked about his change of interest in therapy, and he said it had been helpful but he was feeling better and thought things would improve even more when he was back on the job. He would be too busy for what I then termed a follow-up interview. I nevertheless pressed for one: no fee and at a convenience to his work schedule. He finally agreed and set up the appointment—no-showing two before finally appearing.

At our final meeting he was his original, polite, soft-spoken, respectful self—passive, awaiting my agenda. I asked him what had happened to change his interest in our work. He maintained that nothing had happened and shifted the subject pleasantly into how good he felt being back at work. I permitted him to go on with this for awhile; he emphasized how he had started going out with the guys after work and then he described an "assertion conflict" incident on the assembly line that he had handled better than he had thought he would. Eventually, I directed him back to my contention that something had gone wrong, that perhaps I had said or done something to offend him. At first he protested with much vigor; when I pressed further he recalled that maybe I had sounded sarcastic the last session but it was probably not me, it was himself being too sensitive. I asked for specifics, and he remembered one time when I seemed to have been making fun of the way he kicked the wall when he was mad (this had not been discussed at all the seventh session). I did not correct his mistaken memory—instead I pointed out that I would have appreciated knowing that I had offended him because I did not mean to do so and would have wanted an opportunity to clear it up. He said "yeah, yeah" in an obedient, pressured fashion even as I was speaking and finished with "You're right, I should have." Dismayed at this second error of driving him further into his self-abasing style, I fell silent. He then began treating me, assuring me that he was really OK and how grateful he was—and then he asked his first question about my personal life in a chatty, why–don't–we–change–the–topic way. The session ended in a detached, formal fashion, and at the door I urged him to stay in touch with his uncle.

It might be an oversimplification to propose that a promising therapeutic process fell apart entirely because of one ill-timed joke. Still, it was the only complaint John registered about the therapy, and the content distortion was interesting: his version was thematically related to the actual joke but off the mark enough to suggest that he did not wish to recall it or discuss it openly. Also, from his initial response to the joke (my visual memory of the moment was unusually keen afterward), I ultimately concluded that his laughter had been canned—and that I had misunderstood his response and should have followed up the joke with a query. I had lost contact with the sensitive vulnerability he had displayed in the early sessions and had assumed our relationship was established enough to breach it.

A therapist's introduction of play when the client is "at work" and the presentation of a detached or incongruous angle upon a problem that the client is wrestling with emotionally—both serve to draw the client's attention away from the work rather than facilitate the ongoing processing of information. When the client is in a rut, appears to be treading water, or is otherwise languishing in a stilted intellectual exercise, there may be good reason to interrupt the process in this manner. However, I wrongly concluded that John's long inventory of night spots was such a rut. In retrospect, it seems rather to have been an avoidance maneuver and the levity with which he colored it a form of "whistling in the dark."

Effective therapeutic humor is like a parallel sidetrack to the main route of therapy. It takes the client off the track briefly but does not lose sight of the ongoing themes and allows easy access back to them. While on the sidetrack the client is given a slightly altered view of what is ahead *and* behind. This brief, detached perspective may encourage the client to alter the direction of travel slightly. One of Shakespeare's talents was his ability to weave brief comic asides into the fabric of his tragedies. They not only provided his audience with "comic relief" but typically portended or underscored the drama as it moved toward resolution.

Humor may also sidetrack the client into an entirely new direction and cause the client to lose sight of or access to the original path. The client is subjected to such a radical change of scenery that s/he becomes disoriented and can not integrate it with what had taken place before. It may lead to a derailment, a dead end, or an artificial destination (e.g., a discussion of why the therapist decided to make a joke at that given time).

Searles (1963) has reported a different experience of being "off the track" of humor:

In one session which occurred after we had been working together for several years, she began imitating the various laughs of some six or eight student nurses who were playing and watching tennis on a court outside her window and who, on the eve of their return to their distant home-hospital after having completed their difficult psychiatric affiliation at Chestnut Lodge, were evidently filled with relief and exuberance. The silence of our session was punctuated only by her imitating, from time to time, one or another of the wide variety of laughs which came from the nurses. Her early laughs were done with such "skill" that I thought her genuinely happy, found her laughs often infectious, and laughed with her. But then, as she went on laughing from time to time, the eeriness of what she was doing grew more and more upon me: it became increasingly clear to me that this woman was momentarily hiding her massive despair by imitating laughs for which she, unlike the original authors, had at the moment no correspondingly genuine wellspring of happiness. (p. 48)

This vignette further illustrates the subtlety of "canned laughter" and its ability to mislead. While the outcome of Searles' error was apparently not serious, its occurrence in a relationship several years old attests to the possibility of a "veteran" dyad short-circuiting after an incidence of laughter.

Kubie's paper

In 1971 the *American Journal of Psychiatry* published a paper entitled "The Destructive Potential of Humor in Psychotherapy" by Lawrence Kubie, an eminent and widely-published psychoanalyst. From polite, first-paragraph disclaimers that he did not intend to outlaw humor entirely, Kubie's paper evolved into a bitter diatribe directed at the methods and motivations of bantering therapists. He specifically indicted Harry Stack Sullivan for having abused clients in this manner, and concerning bantering therapists as a group, Kubie offered the following observations:

One is justified in making one generalization about this: Those who are most violent in their defense of humor in psychotherapy often have faces that are distorted with anger even when they think they are at peace and unobserved. Any lecturer on the topic, particularly if the group is not too large, can spot them in the audience by their chronic expressions of tense resentment. These men do not want to be deprived of their right to use and misuse something that they misterm "humor." (p. 866)

His closing paragraph offers a terse conclusion:

> Humor has its place in life. Let us keep it there by acknowledging that one place where it has a very limited role, if any, is in psychotherapy. (p. 866)

Kubie's paper evoked a strong response from the journal's readership (see "Letters to the Editor," *American Journal of Psychiatry*, 1971, 28, p. 118–121). Many psychiatrists were intensely critical of Kubie's position, and some attacked him personally. Kubie's rejoinder (same section) was equally bitter. The highly charged polemics, unusual for a journal of its kind, are interesting *per se*. Unfortunately, they tend to obscure the dangers of humor which Dr. Kubie cogently articulated:

> Consider, for instance, a woman patient who was the last of several children, all but the oldest of whom were brothers. At first she had been a gay and aggressive little tomboy, accepted as such by her older brothers and their friends with praise, pleasure, and indulgence. Inevitably, however, these older brothers and their friends moved on into adolescence, whereupon they did not want the little tomboy anymore but instead a little girl with frills, the very kind of girl whom they had previously looked upon as a "sissy." From that point on they made fun of her tomboy traits, teasing her about that for which they had previously praised her. She developed a rigid intolerance to humor and a serious, crippling defensive-mindedness.
>
> No therapist could have known about this when he was launching her treatment. (When she came to me I had known that she had left two therapists, but I did not know that it was because they had tried unwisely to treat lightly and teasingly the symptoms and fantasies about which she felt so deeply.) She could not have told anyone that she had fled from these two previous efforts to find help because the two therapists had "bantered" in the dark, something, parenthetically, that no therapist has any right to do. Furthermore, these two painful experiences with humorous therapists had made it almost impossible for her to try again, causing her to postpone definitive treatment for years and to bring into her third attempt even greater resistance and defensiveness. (Kubie, 1971, p. 683)

This woman's rejection of the two bantering therapists was not just a transference reaction that emerged from her unique childhood situation. It was also prematurely induced by the therapists' unwitting choices to behave like her older brothers in their efforts to help her change. While childhood teasing has some constructive aspects (Sperling, 1953) and may evolve into an intimacy expression of a mature joking relationship, it frequently leaves scars and resentments when the mixed affiliative-competitive aspects of the teaser-teasee relationship are not resolved. Thus, despite well-meaning intentions and a coherent strategy, the therapist who teases or banters without relevant knowledge concerning a client's early sibling and peer relationships is embarking upon a dangerous course of action.

It would appear that a productive therapeutic alliance had not been established between this woman and either of the two bantering therapists—at least not to a degree where she could freely convey her negative reactions to their methods. One basic element of such an alliance that enables humor to work is the client's trust of the therapist and the therapist's intentions. The absence of interpersonal trust is most remarkable in paranoid conditions; it is worth noting that not a single paper has been written on therapeutic humor with paranoid clients. To the contrary, Sullivan (1949), MacKinnon and Michels (1971), and Rosenheim (1976) have urged clinicians to avoid a humorous attitude with such clients. Paranoid individuals may display a sense of humor toward others; typically this serves as one of many outlets for their bridled hostility. But toward themselves paranoids have little or no sense of humor. MacKinnon and Michels (1971) reported the unfortunate consequences of one such therapist error.

> For example, a paranoid patient made sarcastic, humorous remarks about her physician's scheduling her appointments during the lunch hour. The interviewer misperceived the meaning of the patient's "jokes" and quipped, "The next thing I know you'll be accusing me of trying to starve you." Not long thereafter, the patient developed a delusion that the therapist was plotting her starvation. (p. 289)

Paradoxical methods which appear humorous to an observer or reader have been used successfully with paranoid clients. For example, Jackson (1965) described a successful intervention with a paranoid client who thought that the therapy office was bugged. Jackson's response was to lead the client upon an immediate exploration of "every nook and cranny of the office to find the microphone . . . Following the experience, he plunged meaningfully into a description of his relationship with his wife" (p. 306).

Despite the appearance of humor, such paradoxical interventions (including those associated with Milton Erickson and the Palo Alto group) are not conducted amidst an atmosphere of play, nor are play signals offered by the therapist to induce such an atmosphere. In discussing his work with the paranoid client, Jackson (1963) cautions that "It is, of course, essential that the therapist is sincere in teaching the patient to be more suspicious, else he will humiliate him and ruin the therapy" (p. 307). The ambiguity inherent in paradoxically intervening and simultaneously decommitting from the intervention through the auspices of play is likely to be unsettling (if not traumatizing) to a paranoid individual with severe problems of distrust. In fact, Weeks and L'Abate (1982) have suggested paranoia as a contraindication for any strategy involving paradoxical intervention.

First interviews appear another high risk situation for humor. This statement is not to be construed as a hard-and-fast rule. An effective, first-session intervention by Mindess was discussed earlier (p. 69); Farrelly and Brandsma (1974) acknowledge that their provocative humor may begin in "the first minute of the first interview going for broke at the most available clue" (p. 181). Rosenheim (1974) suggested that a psychodynamic interpretation be made humorously in a first interview as a trial balloon for the therapy process.

Nevertheless, such interventions require one who is both a skilled therapist and a skilled comic. Even if one is able to rule out a tragic teasing history or paranoid trends, the new client's subjective sense of pain and preconceptions of the psychotherapy process are relatively unknown. The novice client likely approaches the first hour with a mixture of desperation, shame, and trepidation; s/he may have acquired scientific and/or religious connotations of the therapist's power and authority from mass media simplifications. S/he may have anxieties garnered from family, friends, or referring sources concerning the peculiar intimacy of psychotherapy: "he must expose all the sensitive areas of his life to a man who does not return the confidences, just as he must talk about all his inadequacies to a man who apparently has none" (Haley, 1963, p. 187). The novice client may also be ambivalent about the financial burden of such a slow, intangible remedy.

None of these factors predispose an individual to a playful frame of mind. Humor about irrelevant, aimless, put–each–other–at–ease topics may facilitate first-session encounters for client and therapist alike. However, the risks of intervening humorously within a relationship of no history are canned or "nervous" laughter to the demand characteristics of the therapist's foreordained power base. If the client is not amused, s/he is unlikely to express this directly.

Another drawback to therapist humor cited by Kubie is that it diverts, arrests, or blocks a client's flow of experience and restricts the range of the client's responses. This criticism is anchored to the psychoanalytic principle that the therapist is not to intrude, distort, nor steer the client's self-presentation. It similarly violates the principles of humanistic therapies which espouse a nondirective approach that will not impinge upon a client's right to self-determine the relationship and shape it in accordance with the client's own personal needs. From a cognitive standpoint, the same observation can be rephrased as disrupting the ongoing flow of information-processing. The holistic (i.e. physiological as well as psychological) nature of laughter, like crying, tends to purge the individual's preexisting state of consciousness. This is apparent in a number of the vignettes discussed earlier in which the authors allude to their clients' reactions which accompany laughter. Poland's client (p. 36) interpreted the therapist's intent to make her laugh; Gerz' client (p. 51) was "shocked." Nelson's executive (p. 65) appeared momentarily confused by her introduction of sarcasm. Roncoli's client (p. 68) hesitated before laughing; my client, John (p. 83), immediately dropped the subject of his anxieties about women. To summarize, the distance inherent to the therapist's humorous intervention and the powerful emotional sequelae which occur when the therapist is "on target"—together, these factors will disrupt the continuity of the ongoing interaction. In some situations (particularly if one is practicing Provocative Therapy) this may be a desirable feature of intervening humorously. In others, particularly when the client is already making productive use of the therapy hour, such an intrusion is difficult to justify.

A final and major concern raised by Kubie is the easy access which humor provides for the distorted expression of countertransference reactions. In addition to hostility and aggression, Kubie warned that novice therapists in particular are likely to alleviate their anxieties about the therapist role through humor. For the nervous beginner, humor provides not only a pleasurable form of denial but also decommitment space if the content of the intervention is subsequently challenged by the client.

Many advocates of humor have effectively neutralized this criticism by pointing out that excessive solemnity can also serve as a defense. Coleman (1971) was even more bitter in rebuking Kubie:

> I have taught the use of banter for many years to beginning students of therapy and have not been impressed with the dangers and dire consequences presented in the article. On the contrary, for the beginner, the use of banter, properly taught, is an exciting experience. It frees him to deal spontaneously and flexibly with the severe problems of character disorder that he is compelled to treat in our teaching clinics, largely because our more senior and experienced therapists approach them no more closely than through the supervisory session. (p. 119)

In his own article on humor, Coleman (1962) stressed that the active role which banter implies for the therapist heightens the therapist's sensitivity and ability to listen to the client. Furthermore, if a casual, friendly atmosphere is maintained, the novice will experience comfort and security in the therapist role. As the client senses this, the therapeutic process is enhanced. In contrast, the traditional recommendation that the student adopt a neutral stance is demanding something "unnatural" of the student; this may occupy the novice's attention at the expense of the client. With typical candor, Greenwald (1967), certainly not a novice, acknowledges that his humorous attitude is "not only for my patients' direct benefit, but also to make it possible for me to deal with their problems without undue suffering" (p. 46). Clearly, Coleman and Greenwald are addressing Kubie's opposition to humor by proposing different conceptions of the therapist role.

Nevertheless, neutralizing Kubie's criticism is not the same as refuting it. And while most discussions have focused upon hostility and anxiety expressed through humor, a wide range of other therapist needs may inadvertently incline one to adopt a humorous perspective: boredom, exhibitionism, seduction, competitiveness. Roncoli (1974) described an ill-advised humorous response made by her to a "promising, intelligent, and attractive young woman." And reviewing my own experience with John, I now view it as more than a coincidence that my sudden adoption of a humorous attitude with him took place during the week following my signing of the publishing contract for this book.

Psychotherapy: A joking relationship?

One assumption for which Kubie may be soundly criticized is his narrow conception of the therapist's role. Consider a sampling of his statements:

> Humor also impairs the therapist's necessary incognito. (p. 864)
> We can maintain this indispensable vigilance only if we remain emotionally objective and uninvolved. (p. 864)
> Yet we hold always to the ultimate question of whether humor facilitates the patient's free associations. (p. 865)

These assertions make clear that while Kubie used the generic term *psychotherapy* throughout his article, he was actually discussing humor from the vantage point of orthodox psychoanalysis. In fact, if one were to substitute the terms *analyst* and *psychoanalysis* for *therapist* and *psychotherapy*, it is doubtful whether the paper would have stirred any controversy. For one who aspires to maximize objectivity and uninvolvement, humor is properly viewed as a "device" (p. 862) and "the sharing of humor (that) automatically creates a powerful secret emotional involvement" (p. 864) as anathema.

At the opposite extreme to Kubie's position is Farrelly's Provocative Therapy in which the therapist adopts the role of devil's advocate. Farrelly's brutal verbal assaults upon his clients understandably affix a reader's attention; the decommitment implied by both his theatric qualifiers (play signals) and the unremitting barrage of his attacks is better appreciated by observing PT. Recall the fact that counterattacks upon the therapist by the client are expected and that the client who does so is viewed as making progress in PT. Taken together, these data suggest that the interpersonal dynamics of PT entail the forging of a joking relationship.

The acknowledged authority on joking relationships is A. R. Radcliffe-Brown, an anthropologist. In two papers written at a time before psychotherapy was an established profession, he documented the existence of formalized joking relationships in a wide variety of cultures at various stages of civilization (Radcliffe-Brown, 1940, 1949). A joking relationship is one in which "privileged disrespect" exists between the participants; one makes a hostile jest at the other's expense, and the receiver/victim is "required" to take no offense. Joking relationships may be symmetrical or asymmetrical. While there are many variations, they tend to involve an individual and an in-law, blood relatives separated by an intervening generation (e.g., grandparents and grandchildren), or blood relatives of adjacent generations who are removed from one another (e.g., uncle and nephew). The common theme underlying the variations is that "The relationship may be said to be one which expresses and emphasizes both detachment (as belonging to separate groups) and attachment (through the indirect personal relations)" (Radcliffe-Brown, 1949, p. 136). It is worth noting here that the psychotherapy relationship also involves a peculiar mixture of intimacy and detachment, what Schofield (1964) termed the "purchase of friendship."

Alford (1981) recently completed a study of joking relationships in American society. He hypothesized that in a complex, industrialized society, the primary significance of joking relationships is their capacity to express feelings of interpersonal intimacy and/or equality within dyadic relationships. His subjects were 206 undergraduate students who were asked to assign ratings of degree of intimacy, relative authority, and frequency of contact within their interpersonal relationships encompassing 34 kin and 12 nonkin categories. He also requested information as to the kind and degree of joking that occurred within each relationship and followed up the survey by conducting extensive interviews with a subsample of 25 of the original questionnaire subjects.

Alford's results revealed that extreme forms of joking (termed "license" and involving mocking disrespect at the receiver's expense) were significantly and positively correlated with high intimacy ratings. With respect to an individual, joking relationships were most likely to be formed with (1) one's parents, (2) one's children, (3) one's siblings, (4) one's spouse, (5) one's best friend, (6) one's roommates, (7) one's coworkers, and (8) one's same-sex work superiors. Most of the above relationships involved a perceived equal status between the participants; in the cases of parents and work supervisors, Alford concluded that high intimacy and high frequency of contact countered the effects of inequality between the participants. His overall conclusion was that "joking relationships are symbolic markers of intimacy and/or relative equality in both preindustrial and industrial societies . . . they constitute a play form predominantly engaged in by intimate equals" (Alford, 1981, p. 4).

These data are not cited to suggest a preferred new direction of psychotherapeutic practice. But they do support the notion that critical humor can serve as an intimacy language for therapists and clients who are well versed in this idiom of alliance and self-expression. As Coleman (1962) wrote:

> Banter is the most significant form of affectionate interchange in groups. In groups of high morale—where the ambivalent feelings toward the leader are in balance—banter is the major medium for the transmission and dissemination of an affectionate steady state. There are few individuals in our society who have not, at one time or another, had the gratifying experience of group belonging and its ritual-like validation through banter. This kind of experience creates a readiness to respond to banter with feelings of uninvolved affection, or rather of affectionate binding in which there is no personal commitment. (p. 72)

The litmus test of whether a therapist-client dyad is engaged in the formation of a productive joking relationship (as opposed to a one-upmanship game or worse) resides in the therapist's reaction to being victimized. If the therapist's laughter is one of affectionate recognition that his/her foibles (humanity) are evident to the client, and both members of the dyad understand their relationship as one of intimate equals who are connected but not involved, the sham conflicts and attacks of critical humor celebrate the shared insight "I'm not OK—you're not OK—but that's OK." (Mindess, 1976).

There are obvious difficulties in forging such a relationship and difficulties in its maintenance. The maintenance danger is not that the participants will eventually alienate one another but that the boundaries between them will dissolve entirely and the working purpose underlying the relationship's formation will be lost in the sea of play. There has been much attention devoted recently to sexual encounters between therapists and clients and the adverse effects upon all concerned. While the nature and extent of this problem are not fully understood, it is doubtful whether every instance can be reduced to a therapist authoritarianly exploiting the client.

In conclusion, there is every reason to believe that a joking relationship between intimate equals can be therapeutic despite the manifest auspices of attack/counterattack. The establishment and maintenance of such a relationship appears more in the realm of the art of psychotherapy than in its science at this time. But this statement applies equally to the more traditional forms of therapeutic relatedness.

One psychiatrist wrote the following in response to Kubie's article: "The appropriateness of using humor depends more on the therapist-patient fit and on the therapist's sensitivity than it does on absolute factors inherent in humor" (Friedman, 1971, p. 118). The only questionable part of this statement is the existence of absolute factors inherent in humor.

Chapter 7

Special Topics

Child therapy

One must be cautious in making any general statements about the therapeutic potential of humor among a population so psychologically diverse as "children." Amusing stimulus structures which pose an effective cognitive challenge are far more sophisticated and complex for the 11-year-old than those which work with the 4-year-old. By the same token, the preadolescent and the preschooler are invested in different socialization and identity dilemmas; hence the motivational sources of humor in effective joke content also vary greatly between the two groups. For a review of the developmental issues in humor from a cognitive perspective, the reader is referred to McGhee (1979). Wolfenstein (1954) has provided the most comprehensive review of motivational theme changes in children's humor from a psychoanalytic standpoint.

Nevertheless, it appears safe to conclude that a therapist's sense of humor integrates more easily in working with children than with adults. The major reason is that a humorous attitude as a vehicle of thought, self-expression, and communication is more easily adopted and understood by children. Children have more day-to-day experience in this mode than adults, and younger ones, particularly preschoolers, spend a majority of their time in non-goal-oriented, activity-for-activity's-sake pursuits. Humor is a form of mental play, and children readily acclimate to the playful frame of mind. A therapist who readily adopts and relates to a child through this state is practicing a form of global empathy that is likely to further any theme or relationship formation process at hand.

As is the case with adult therapy, there is currently little empirical data as to the quantity and quality of humor in child therapy. Orfanidis (1972) tape recorded sessions of therapy involving 10 children between the ages of 7 and 10. While her paper focuses upon humor themes and styles of individual children rather than a statistical analysis of humor parameters within her sample, she does report that 75 percent of the humorous interactions between child and therapist were initiated by the child. Such a finding raises the question of whether humor is a preferred form of resistance by children: an attempt to draw the therapist out of the doctor role and into the playmate realm of fantasy, make-believe, and "let's pretend."

All child therapists who have addressed this question agree that this resistance interpretation commonly applied to adult humor is not valid with children. Tolor (1966) observed that children seldom jest or joke with their therapists in the early stages of therapy when their anxiety levels are greatest; rather, humor emerges after a positive transference to the therapist is established. Yorukoglu (1974) endorsed this observation, adding that a child's humor "may also be viewed as part of the child's contribution to the therapeutic alliance" (p. 678). Shaw (1961) went further in venturing that a child is more open and revealing in a humorous atmosphere: "He seems to feel he is on safer ground, that there is a kind of pact between him and the examiner, that here is a person who can meet him on his own level" (p. 374). Collectively, these writers are suggesting that children may seek to form a variant of a joking relationship with their therapists. This is not surprising, particularly with respect to younger children whose unstructured interactions with adults (and peers) are predominantly colored by playful rather than goal-oriented behaviors.

Another reason why humor may be more welcomed by and effective with children is the fact that children seldom (if ever) volunteer for therapy. They are led or forced into therapy by their parents who tend to have the worried, desperate, this-is-our-only-hope sort of feelings previously discussed as inimical to a humorous atmosphere. But the coerced child does not share these feelings; the child is more likely to be anxious, withdrawn, and apprehensive about the "special doctor" whose role s/he neither welcomes nor understands. The child may conceive of therapy as a punishment for something s/he has done wrong, or with a fear fueled by recollections of doctors who had given painful shots in the past. There may be a whole host of other idiosyncratic fears and associations; it is thus likely that a child's entrance into therapy as a nonvolunteer will be characterized by start-up feelings of fear and avoidance, perhaps oppositionalism. To then encounter a therapist who is readily whimsical, who jokes, kids, or plays light teasing games and thus speaks in a language readily understood by the child—this will allay the child's anxieties and facilitate the beginnings of a productive relationship. Adults, of course, have related fears of therapy. However, the act of volunteering implies that these fears have been partially or temporarily mastered or are outweighed by the need to find someone who can listen and help. Thus the social lubricating functions of humor are less important with adults than with children and, in some cases, may be inappropriate.

Turning from general to specific applications of humor with children, Yorukoglu (1974) has espoused the favorite joke technique discussed earlier (pp. 27–30). Many of his observations and conclusions are identical to those of Zwirling (1955); one innovation available in child work is to relate the child's favorite joke to the parents in a separate interview format. Yorukoglu asserts that, when done with the child's consent, this is an excellent method of helping the anxious, perplexed parents to empathize with their child: "In most instances they grasped the truth behind the joke right away . . . their resistance to the therapist's later suggestions was minimized" (p. 689). When one is able to offer parents a concrete, revealing, and evocative piece of their child's psychology, their participation as cotherapists is fostered more readily than when one is forced to rely upon empty adjectives or technical language.

One foundation of play therapy is the premise that children do not have a sufficient vocabulary or the verbal facility to communicate their internal experience through words. Shaw

(1961) provided a revealing example of how a humorous interlude with a nine-year-old boy helped to supply him with the verbal means to express differing degrees of hostility toward various family members:

Q: Now, John, just imagine that you are 19 years old, a tackle on the Michigan football team, with muscles this big, and your father comes up to you and says, "John, get to bed immediately." What would you do?

A [*Grinning widely, savoring the scene to the fullest*]: I'd hit him.

Q: And how far would you knock him?

A: About two feet.

Q: And how far would you knock mother if *she* told you to get to bed?

A [*Gleefully*]: About five feet!

Q: And how far would you knock big brother?

A: Oh, I wouldn't even hit him at all. (p. 374)

Consistent with the research findings of Jacob Levine, Paul McGhee, Martha Wolfenstein, and others, child therapists stress that children's humor during the therapy hour provides a key to understanding the conflicts they are attempting to master. For example, one of the clients from Orfanidis' (1972) sample was a boy who had been given the distressing news that he was to endure a school transfer in the upcoming academic year. The child worked through his immediate feelings about the transfer by humorously attacking his therapist:

Johnny: You're retarded! You're goin' in the retarded room. Whenever I lose a game you don't win because retarded guys can't win . . . You're not retarded, but you sure act like it! They'll close you up . . . They'll tape you for being retarded. You say I'm retarded . . . you're more retarded than I am . . . You aren't retarded, but you sure talk retarded. Ask anybody else. What will they say? . . . Guess what they'll say! [*Mimicking*] "Retarded!"

Therapist: I'm retarded?

Johnny: Yes . . . I'm not retarded [*giggle*].

Johnny [*A while later*]: If you stop talking, maybe you won't be so retarded. [Then Johnny expressed concern that his therapist might discontinue treatment with him.]

Therapist: You'll still see me.

Johnny: That's good, because I might get a *real* dumb guy.

Therapist: Even dumber than me?

Johnny: You aren't dumb, but I'll get a real dumb guy! (Orfanidis, 1972, p. 152)

Following his transparent projection onto the therapist, Johnny's giggle represents a mastery pivot as it follows his assertion of not being retarded. In the remainder of the excerpt, his concerns about retardation are relegated to the background as his center-stage focus becomes one of undoing the initial projection. One must conclude that his humor provided him with at least short-term respite from his anxieties surrounding his school transfer.

There are two case reports in the literature which indicate that allowing free reign to a child's sense of humor can lead to substantial therapeutic benefit. Loewald (1976) detailed many humorous interactions which occurred in her year-long treatment of a four-year-old boy who presented with severe difficulties in handling aggression. Initially there had been no indications that the boy was particularly gifted with a sense of humor, but he rapidly adopted this medium with a therapist who chose to permit it: "His teasing—expressing both hostile resistance and the wish for closeness—was pleasurable for both of us. And it maintained the certain degree of separateness, detachment, with which Cy seemed comfortable. In the teasing 'joke' he had evolved a mastering behavior for reexperiencing separation and reunion over and over again" (Loewald, 1976, p. 211). In discussing the positive outcome, Loewald emphasized the sublimation functions of Cy's humor as it manifested itself through the final termination interview.

Domash (1975) reported her treatment of a borderline psychotic boy of 9½ whose sense of humor proceeded through three distinct phases as it mirrored the progress of the therapy. In the early, "out-of-contact" phase, the boy relied upon humor to fend off the therapist's attempts to relate with him. In the second, relationship-formation phase, the dyad evolved a joking relationship in which the boy took the role of comic and Domash became his "straight man." In the third phase their relationship solidified; the boy's reliance on humor decreased as he began to confide in his therapist more openly and directly. The author reached conclusions similar to those of Nelson (p. 63–66) about humor and borderline characters: "It is suggested here that in borderline states, if wit appears, it can be used as a strengthening device, in contrast to neurotic patients who might use wit as a resistance" (Domash, 1975, p. 262).

Family therapy

Among the leaders of the family therapy movement, only Salvador Minuchin has specifically acknowledged a role for humor in treatment. The vignette which follows involved a 14-year-old boy who was being treated in a day hospital program for depression and truancy. Minuchin was interviewing the boy and his parents for the first time in a consultation role. The interview had begun with the mother opening up the problem of her son (Bud) not getting out of bed in the morning early enough to arrive at the day hospital on time. Minuchin's initial response was to turn his back to the mother and address Bud. His initial statements to the boy had normalized the problem by reframing Bud as a "night person."

Bud: Not real late. It's just in the morning that I don't feel like doing anything.

Minuchin: But that means that you feel more active in the evening.

Bud: No, I feel active all day, but—

Minuchin: If you had a good alarm clock, would that solve it?

Bud: Well, the alarm clock I've got now—

Minuchin: Who is the alarm clock?

Bud: Well, I've got one of my own.

Minuchin: Do you have an alarm clock, or is mother an alarm clock?

Bud: I've got one.

Mother: And I've got one.

Minuchin: Are you certain she's not an alarm clock, Bud?

Bud: Yes.

Minuchin: Who wakes you up?

Bud: She does most of the time.

Minuchin: So, she's your alarm clock.

Mother: If you want to call it that.

Minuchin: Okay, so you have a function. You are an alarm clock!

Mother: Well, at the present time, we have two alarm clocks in his bedroom—

Minuchin: And they don't work?

Mother: And me.

Minuchin: That means, maybe, you could put on a third alarm, staggered, like one at 7:30, one at 7:40, one at 7:50.

Mother: That's how I work it now.

Minuchin: My goodness! You must be a very deep sleeper, Bud.

Bud: Yeah.

Minuchin: I got up today at four o'clock in the morning. I couldn't sleep. I wish I could get your symptom. If your three alarm clocks don't work, you can sleep until 12 o'clock, 1 o'clock, 2 o'clock—what's the latest that you have been able to keep sleeping?

Bud: [*Looks at mother*]

Minuchin: Don't ask her. That is not her function. She's an alarm clock. Is she also a memory bank? (Minuchin & Fishman, 1981, p. 43–44)

Minuchin described his interview style during this excerpt as light banter. He acknowledged that his interventions with the family were unusually active and fast-paced for a first interview but justified them by his own sense of comfort at the time, a sense that he was in "the permissible range." There is objective evidence to support this in the mother's agreement to accept his interpretation of her being Bud's alarm clock.

Minuchin's structural approach to family therapy views the family as an "organism" with a unique homeostatic balance among its individual members. The therapist's task is to restructure the organism by changing the chemistry and mechanics of its homeostasis. A strategy of this approach which is particularly relevant to humor is the therapist's "joining" the family to create a new social unit. When this is achieved, the therapist becomes a member of the in-group with permission to engage in the subtle, personalized banter and "inside jokes" that, coming from outside the group, would be viewed by the group as an attack upon one (or more) of its members.

"Joining" a family in this sense is probably more art than science. And Minuchin's brand of humor is not a shrill, caustic one. At various times he refers to his sense of humor as soft, light, gentle, and compassionate: "I have learned to use my life experiences and my fellow feeling for families as part of the therapeutic process. Having made my share of mistakes in my life, I don't expect my patients to be perfect. I know that family members do the best they can, and that sometimes the results are very destructive" (Minuchin & Fishman, 1981, p. 289). Note also in the vignette above that Minuchin's banter is lightly critical of both mother and son at various points. Side-taking is an acceptable tactic to unbalance a disturbed family's homeostasis, but it is a flexible mode of intervention and does not extend to the formation of an entrenched alliance with one family member against the others. When the therapist's banter is directed toward all members at various times, it can be viewed as a language of challenge among an in-group seeking to reorganize itself.

In family therapy systems in which the therapist does not join the family in forming a "we-group," the applicability of humor is correspondingly minimized. For example, the Palo Alto group spearheaded by Gregory Bateson has played a prominent theoretical role in the origins of family therapy. In various publications (Bateson, Jackson, Haley, & Weakland, 1956; Watzlawick, 1963; Fry, 1963) humor has been offered as an example of a metacommunication vehicle which violates the theory of logical types; similar metacommunication processes are central to the Palo Alto conception of family pathology. Despite its allegiance to paradoxical tactics, the strategic approach to family therapy which emerged from this group is not one to emphasize humor. Watzlawick (et al., 1974; 1978) has recently alluded to therapeutic properties of humor, but these are allusions only.

Compared to Minuchin's approach, the therapist's role in strategic family therapy is one of detached participation which precludes a "we-ness" with the family. Paradoxical interventions are made in earnest, without play signals. That laughter is a common reaction to a paradoxical intervention (Weeks & L'Abate, 1982) does not define it as humor if its sender meant otherwise. Rather, laughter in this instance must be viewed as a type of resistance that is peculiarly common to paradoxical strategies: the therapist provides the "apparent" humor stimulus, and the client responds with a play signal (his/her own laughter) which asks "You were joking, right?" If the therapist subsequently laughs, s/he accomplishes a total decommitment from the intervention by agreeing to cast it into the realm of play. A slight smile, on the other hand, may communicate an empathic, partial decommitment ("I can see how that's hard for you to take seriously") without mitigating the spirit of the intervention entirely.

Inappropriate laughter (i.e., laughter in the absence of apparent humor stimulus and play signal) is common among families in treatment, and to interpret such laughter as mere tension reduction may be myopic. In a series of papers, Gerald Zuk (et al., 1963, 1964, 1966) articulated various system dynamics that can be applied to such laughter. The following excerpt is from a family interview involving a schizophrenic woman and her parents. The issue under discussion was whether the daughter would be able to move out of her parents' home, even after marriage:

Mother: You want to live with us or you want to live alone?

Patient: I don't know. Before I wanted to live in the neighborhood, you know.

Mother: Now you wouldn't want to live with us—you want to live alone?

Patient: Yeah.

Mother: It's better to live alone than to live with the mother after you're married, you know.

Patient: Everybody's different. [*More laughter here from the patient*]

Therapist [*To mother*]:   But would you be able to take that big loss? [*Mother begins to giggle and laugh in response to this comment. Patient then joins her mother in laughter.*] You're laughing just like your daughter was. I don't understand why both of you are laughing.

Mother: I don't know what you mean by big loss? What am I going to do—if she gets married? (Zuk, 1964, p. 79)

Clearly there is no therapist intent to be humorous in this vignette, and the content of the therapist's remarks have no amusement potential. The remarks do have anxiety-arousing properties, however, and the mother's giggle represents an attempt to ward-off the anxiety (or master it, depending upon one's theoretical persuasion). What is different and problematic in this family context (as opposed to an individual therapy one) is the daughter's joining in with the mother in laughter. While further validating the therapist's line of inquiry, the daughter's laughter also supports the mother's laugh-it-off resistance, and as a colluding dyad they are in a better position to thwart any further attempts of the therapist to focus on the symbiotic aspects of their relationship. The therapist's next comment attests to a state of puzzlement understandable for any "outsider." Throughout this and other sections of the vignette, the mother-daughter dyad eludes a meaningful confrontation with their symbiosis issue by laughing at its initial appearance and flitting away in laughter's aftermath.

Citing this case among others (see particularly Zuk et al., 1963), the author argues convincingly that "inappropriate" laughter by family members represents a covert communication to qualify and disguise the meaning of what has been presented to the therapist as "outsider." It thus serves in-group self-maintenance functions and "may be an important prop in the maintenance of the pathological double-bind system, as well as other pathological systems" (Zuk, 1964, p. 88).

This points up some unique issues for the family therapist who might apply his/her sense of humor in treatment. Unless the therapist is integrated within the "we group," humor, particularly of the critical variety, may have insidious effects upon the therapist-family relationship. In addition to the sender and receiver there is an audience which is more closely involved (positively or negatively) with the receiver. Secret alliances within the in-group, the many ramifications of side-taking, and the dynamics of humor originating from an outsider—all of these factors make humor a difficult tactic to monitor and guide effectively in a family therapy context.

Group therapy

Many of the group dynamics affecting humor amidst a family apply to the group therapy setting as well. One key difference is that the group therapist is not confronting a we-group of some years history. Instead, the therapist is seeking to forge a we-group among a group of individuals who had no relationships with one another previously. Various approaches to group therapy diverge in their stances as to what extent the therapist should gravitate toward the leader versus the peer side of the we-group or to what extent the therapist should vacillate between these two poles. Nevertheless, all group therapy approaches agree that the therapist is never to function as an aloof, detached outsider nor be perceived that way by other group members. There may be ephemeral processes in the history of any cohesive group in which the other members direct hostility toward the therapist (Yalom, 1970) or try to symbolically expel the therapist. But one steady perception of the therapist by the members is that s/he is the group's *raison d'être* and the congealing force in the group's continuing existence. The family therapist works within a much different cohesion context.

Grotjahn (1971a, 1971b, 1977) has argued that a sense of humor is an important quality for any group therapist. In his view it is a major safeguard against the "infantilization" of the group (i.e., the leader becomes so distantly authoritarian and parental as to become an outsider). The therapist's sense of humor further serves to correct "transference distortions" and counteracts secret fantasies among group members as to the therapist's omnipotence. He applauded the therapist's rich laughter upon being made the butt of a wisecrack in the following circumstance:

> It was the therapist's habit to be on time or even 10 minutes early, so that he could open the doors between his waiting room and his consultation room to watch the group assemble, which often gave him valuable clues to the interaction that followed. Once the therapist came shooting into the office at the last minute, and the group commented about it. One of the men looked sternly at him and said:
> "I assume you had a motorboat accident while taking your morning walk?" (Grotjahn, 1971, p. 760)

In addition to enjoying the member's sarcasm, Grotjahn urges that the therapist be mindful of the "walk on water" content theme implied by such a remark. In laughing, the therapist quickly cancels any allegiance to being imbued with Christlike powers.

Bloch, Browning, and McGrath (1983) asserted that the group therapist's ready sense of humor serves modeling functions for the members and that the human-ness so displayed promotes the process of group cohesion.

> In the course of such a marathon, as the participants ate together during a break, one of the cotherapists dealt good-humouredly and amusingly with the mess he had made with a juicy pear. Several patients were surprised that this potentially embarrassing social situation could be so light-heartedly mastered, and proceeded to eat their own food with less self-consciousness. (p. 90)

Even as there are cogent arguments that the group therapist should promote and join in situations of group humor to foster cohesion, s/he should not do so unconsciously. At times

the group's laughter may represent a collective effort to dispose
of an anxiety-arousing issue. There may be cohesion in resistance and avoidance. Kris (1940) observed "in a group-situation
one may join in the laugh without quite knowing what the
laughter is all about . . . At this point laughter is not necessarily
a reaction to a common stimulus. The laughter of the group no
longer requires a 'butt' to laugh at, it can itself represent both
content and sealing of the pact. The motive for laughing will
sink into the background in this way, as the mass-tie becomes
sufficiently strengthened, at the same time that the controlling
and inhibiting function of the individual becomes restricted"
(p. 319). These notions are identical to those of LeBon (1896)
in his famous treatise on the psychology of crowds. With its
physiological basis, laughter in a group setting has a contagion
power when an anxious subject applies to all—just as anger may
take over a group and transform it into a lynch mob. Consider
the following vignette from Vargas (1961):

> In a group discussion a woman revealed how she had used
> the "menopause" to get away with some of her complaints at
> home. Others in the group were much amused and they also
> began to reveal how they had misused the "menopause" as a way
> of getting away with things that they didn't think they would be
> permitted otherwise. As each woman stated her use of the
> "menopause" more and more serious problems were revealed,
> and more and more injustices and disturbing conditions were
> explored and yet each deeper revelation was greeted with in-
> creasing hilarity. (p. 200)

This sort of nonhumorous laughter (i.e., without play signals nor an identifiable humor stimulus) suggests revelation
and resistance with the validity of the opened issue being canceled by laughter into the realm of play. A group therapist may
choose to confront the group with its laughter or formulate a
group interpretation as to the meaning of menopause. Another
option is to wait until the laughter subsides and invite a serious
discussion of menopause; still another is simply to wait in silence
and allow the group members to determine a future direction.
Any or all of these tactical options would apply in various systems. But joining heartily into the laughter and perhaps adding
one's own confession about menopause is clearly contra-
indicated. To do so would represent a public abdication of one's
role as therapist within the group. In other instances, when
there is a chain of jokes and wisecracks accompanied by obvious

play signals, the therapist may appropriately elect to join the play atmosphere. Such play periods foster universality and cohesion among group members.

Once the therapist's role is well defined and the group has evolved into a cohesive working alliance, many of the humorous intervention styles discussed earlier in connection with individual therapy may apply (Vargas, 1961; Hankins-McNary, 1979; Bloch, Browning, & McGrath, 1983). In addition, the group therapist may witness other members intervening humorously with one another. In the following vignette (Bloch, Browning, & McGrath, 1983) the group treated an individual member by shifting from an earnest to a light perspective on a newly revealed problem:

> She described an episode in which she had been visited by a boyfriend who invited her out. On Mary's refusal he assumed the role of "counsellor," very much outstayed his welcome, and tried to persuade her to "talk about it." This was the first occasion that her problems of sexuality and relations with men had been explicitly raised in the group. The result was a catalogue of practical advice but no effort to explore the more basic issues involved. As more details of their awkward and embarrassing evening emerged, its "soap-opera" quality became increasingly apparent and the mood of the group shifted from serious and practical to good-humoured and bantering. Mary, caught between distress and amusement, perceived some of the ridiculousness of the situation and the attempts to solve her problems through rather naive practical suggestions. She was then able to reappraise her problems and following her lead the group was better placed to examine in collaboration with Mary her ambivalence towards her sexuality. (p. 92)

The following vignette, which took place in a military inpatient setting (Wilmer, 1958), illustrates how a group member's wit directed at another member may also address group-wide issues of universality and cohesion:

> A similar instance occurred in a meeting where a "psychopathic" Marine was acting the role of a visiting sniper who did not really belong to the group. Another patient, with an obvious reference to the Marine and to the popular view of the Marines as "elite" of the military service, said, "If you were all right you wouldn't be in this elite group." This remark evoked considerable laughter, and it had a distinctly leveling effect on the patients who acted as if they didn't belong. (p. 274)

Critical humor thus may have meanings and implications that extend beyond the sender-receiver dyad in a group. In other instances such sarcastic interchanges among members may not be so growth-promoting. Instead, they may be directed toward the social alienation of one member (the receiver) from the rest of the group, as when certain members tire quickly of the constant antics of a member who plays the clown, the help-rejecting complainer, etc. In such situations the therapist must consider the advisability not only of rescuing the victim but also of preventing the group's splitting into two factions that may align behind the sender and the receiver-victim.

Afterthoughts

Hopefully at this point the reader is convinced that notions of humor as tension-reduction or comic relief are oversimplifications; that generalizing from one instance of humor to another is inappropriate in most cases; that an instance of humor shared during a therapy hour is worthy of a second thought; that humor is not fundamentally a defense mechanism/resistance or fundamentally a panacea.

The current trend, within the psychotherapy professions and without, is toward viewing humor on the panacea side of the spectrum. Within the professions one source of this trend is the growing disillusionment spawned by theoretical orthodoxies which had, over the years, reified into different versions of "the truth." Another is the increase in the number of psychotherapy consumers; as caseloads have expanded, the stress and strain upon professional listeners has increased, yielding the current interest in the concept of "burnout." Outside of the professions, the holistic health movement is shaping perceptions of laughter and humor. There are general cultural trends away from pollution, preservatives, and pills toward a clean environment, natural foods, and physical and spiritual fitness. As psychotherapists and citizens, we must share in such changes, participate in them, promote them—but do so in a manner that is mindful of the dangers of excess and religiosity.

Finally, humor research to this point has suffered from "multidisciplinary-itis." Psychoanalysis has focused upon humor content, psychology upon stimulus structures and humor responses. Sociologists have studied humor in group definition processes while anthropologists have focused upon cultural functions of humor. The unfortunate outcome is piecemeal knowledge which resists integration. A more interdisciplinary spirit is called for; the initiation of a series of international conferences on humor and laughter (Cardiff, Wales 1976; Los Angeles, 1980; Washington, D. C., 1982; Tel Aviv, 1984) represents a step in this direction.

References

Alford, F. The joking relationship in American society. *American Humor*, 1981, *8*, 1–8.

Alford, F. *The evolutionary significance of the human humor response.* Paper presented to the Third International Conference on Humor, Washington, D.C., August 1982.

Allport, G. W. *The individual and his religion.* New York: Holt, Rinehart & Winston, 1950.

Allport, G. W. *Pattern and growth in personality.* New York: Holt, Rinehart & Winston, 1961.

Ansell, C., Mindess, H., et al. Pies in the face and similar matters. *Voices*, 1981, *16*, 10–24.

Apter, M. J., & Smith, K. C. P. Humour and the theory of psychological reversals. In A. J. Chapman & H. C. Foot (Eds.), *It's a funny thing, humour.* Oxford, U.K.: Pergamon, 1977, 95–101.

Bateson, G., Jackson, D., Haley, J., & Weakland, J. Toward a theory of schizophrenia. *Behavioral Science*, 1956, *1*, 251–264.

Bellak, L., Hurvich, M., & Gediman, H. K. *Ego functions in schizophrenics, neurotics, and normals.* New York: John Wiley & Sons, 1973.

Berlyne, D. E. *Conflict, arousal, and curiosity.* New York: McGraw-Hill, 1960.

Berlyne, D. E. Humor and its kin. In J. H. Goldstein & P. E. McGhee (Eds.), *The psychology of humor.* New York: Academic Press, 1972, 43–60.

Bloch, S., Browning, S., & McGrath, G. Humour in group psychotherapy. *British Journal of Medical Psychology*, 1983, *56*, 89–97.

Caplan, G. *Principles of preventive psychiatry*. New York: Basic Books, 1964.

Chapman, A. J., & Foot, H. C. Introduction. In A. J. Chapman & H. C. Foot (Eds.), *Humour and laughter: Theory, research, and applications*. London: John Wiley & Sons, Ltd., 1976, 1–7.

Coleman, J. V. Banter as psychotherapeutic intervention. *American Journal of Psychoanalysis*, 1962, *22*, 69–74.

Coleman, J. V. Comment on "The destructive potential of humor in psychotherapy" by Lawrence Kubie. *American Journal of Psychiatry*, 1971, *128*, 119.

Cousins, N. *The anatomy of an illness*. New York: W. W. Norton, 1979.

Dean, A. *It's a long way to heaven*. New York: Simon & Schuster, 1949.

Domash, L. The use of wit and the comic by a borderline psychotic child in psychotherapy. *American Journal of Psychotherapy*, 1975, *29*, 261–270.

Ellis, A. *Humanistic psychotherapy: The rational-emotive approach*. New York: Julian Press, 1973.

Ellis, A. Fun as psychotherapy. *Rational Living*, 1977, *12*, 2–6.

Farrelly, F., & Brandsma, J. *Provocative therapy*. Cupertina, Calif.: Meta Publications, 1974.

Farrelly, F., & Matthews, S. Provocative therapy. In R. Corsini (Ed.), *Innovative psychotherapies*. New York: John Wiley & Sons, 1981, 678–693.

Fenichel, O. *The psychoanalytic theory of neurosis*. New York: W. W. Norton, 1945.

Ferreira, A. J. Psychotherapy with severely regressed schizophrenics. *Psychiatric Quarterly*. 1959, *33*, 663–682

Fine, H. J., Pollio, H. R. & Simpkinson, C. H. Figurative language, metaphor, and psychotherapy. *Psychotherapy: Theory, Research, & Practice*, 1973, *10*, 87–91.

Fisher S., & Fisher, R. L. *Pretend the world is funny and forever: A psychological analysis of comedians, clowns, and actors*. Hillsdale, N.J.: Lawrence Erlbaum Associates, 1981.

Frankl, V. E. Paradoxical intention: A logotherapeutic technique. In V. E. Frankl, et al., *Psychotherapy and existentialism*. New York: Washington Square Press, 1967.

Frankl, V. E. [*The doctor and the soul* (2nd ed.)] (R. Winston & C. Winston, trans.). New York: Alfred A. Knopf, copyright 1968.

Freud, S. *Jokes and their relation to the unconscious*. New York: W. W. Norton, 1960. (Originally *Der Witz und seine Beziehung zum Uhewussten*. Leipzig & Vienna: Deuticke, 1905.)

Freud, S. Humour. In *Collected papers, volume V*. New York: Basic Books, 1957. (Originally, *International Journal of Psychoanalysis*, 1928, *9*, 1–6.)

Friedman, H. J. Comment on "The destructive potential of humor in psychotherapy" by Lawrence Kubie. *American Journal of Psychiatry*, 1971, *128*, 118.

Fromm-Reichmann, F. *Principles of intensive psychotherapy*. Chicago: University of Chicago Press, 1950.

Fry, W. F. *Sweet madness.* Palo Alto, Calif.: Pacific Books, 1963.

Gerz, H. O. The treatment of the phobic and the obsessive-compulsive patient using paradoxical intention sec. Viktor E. Frankl. *Journal of Neuropsychiatry,* 1962, *3,* 375–387.

Getzels, J. W., & Jackson, P. W. *Creativity and intelligence.* New York: John Wiley & Sons, 1962.

Goldstein, J. H., Suls, J. M., & Anthony, S. Enjoyment of specific types of humor content: Motivation or salience? In J. H. Goldstein & P. E. McGhee (Eds.), *The psychology of humor.* New York: Academic Press, 1972, 159–172.

Goldstein, J. H., Harman, J., McGhee, P. E., & Karasik, R. Test of an information-processing model of humor: Physiological response changes during problem and riddle solving. *Journal of General Psychology,* 1975, *92,* 59–68.

Goldstein, J. H. Theoretical notes on humor. *Journal of Communication,* 1976, *26,* 104–112.

Goldstein, J. H. A laugh a day: Can mirth keep disease at bay? *The Sciences,* 1982, *22,* 21–25.

Greenson, R. R. *The technique and practice of psychoanalysis.* London: Hogarth Press, 1967.

Greenwald, H. Play therapy for children over twenty-one. *Psychotherapy: Theory, Research, and Practice,* 1967, 44–46.

Greenwald, H. Humor in psychotherapy. *Journal of Contemporary Psychotherapy,* 1975, *7,* 113–116.

Grossman, S. A. The use of sexual jokes in psychotherapy. *Medical Aspects of Human Sexuality,* 1970, *4,* 35–46.

Grossman, S. A. The use of jokes in psychotherapy. In A. J. Chapman & H. C. Foot (Eds.), *It's a funny thing, humour.* Oxford, U.K.: Pergamon, 1977, 144–153.

Grotjahn, M. Laughter in psychoanalysis. *Samiksa* (Journal of the Indian Psycho-Analytic Society, Calcutta), 1949, *3,* 76–82.

Grotjahn, M. *Beyond laughter.* New York: McGraw-Hill, 1956.

Grotjahn, M. Laughter in psychotherapy. In W. M. Mendel (Ed.), *A celebration of laughter.* Los Angeles: Mara Books, 1970, 61–66.

Grotjahn, M. Laughter in group psychotherapy. *International Journal of Group Psychotherapy,* 1971, *21,* 234–238. (a)

Grotjahn, M. The qualities of the group therapist. In H. I. Kaplan & B. J. Sadock (Eds.), *Comprehensive group psychotherapy.* Baltimore: Williams & Wilkins, 1971, p. 757–774. (b)

Grotjahn, M. *The art and technique of analytic group therapy.* New York: Jason Aronson, 1977.

Haley, J. *Strategies of psychotherapy.* New York: Grune & Stratton, 1963.

Haley, J. *Problem-solving therapy.* San Francisco: Jossey-Bass, 1978.

Halpern, H. M. The right joke. *Voices,* 1969, *5,* 54–56.

Hankins-McNary, L. The use of humor in group therapy. *Perspectives in Psychiatric Care,* 1979, *17,* 228–231.

Heuscher, J. E. The role of humor and folklore themes in psychotherapy. *American Journal of Psychiatry*, 1980, *137*, 1546–1549.

Hickson, J. Humor as an element in the counseling relationship. *Psychology*, 1977, *14*, 60–68.

Hobbs, N. Sources of gain in psychotherapy. *American Psychologist*, 1962, *17*, 741–747.

Jackson, D. D. A suggestion for the technical handling of paranoid patients. *Psychiatry*, 1963, *26*, 306–307.

Janus, S. S. The great comedians: Personality and other factors. *American Journal of Psychoanalysis*, 1975, *35*, 169–174.

Kaczanowski, G. Logotherapy—A new psychotherapeutic tool. *Psychosomatics*, 1967, *8*, 158–161.

Kadis, A. L., & Winick, C. The cartoon as therapeutic catalyst. In H. H. Mosak (Ed.), *Alfred Adler: His influence on psychology today*. Park Ridge, N.J.: Noyes Press, 1973, 106–123.

Kane, T. R., Suls, J. M., & Tedeschi, J. Humour as a tool of social interaction. In A. J. Chapman & H. C. Foot (Eds.), *It's a funny thing, humour*. Oxford, U.K.: Pergamon, 1977, 13–17.

Keith-Spiegel, P. Preface to symposium proceedings. *Social aspects of humor: Recent research and theory*. Western Psychological Association Meeting, Vancouver, 1969.

Keith-Spiegel, P. Early conceptions of humor: Varieties and issues. In J. H. Goldstein & P. E. McGhee (Eds.), *The psychology of humor*. New York: Academic Press, 1972, 4–42.

Kernberg, O. F. *Borderline conditions and pathological narcissism*. New York: Aronson, 1975.

Killinger, B. E. *The place of humour in adult psychotherapy*. Unpublished doctoral dissertation, York University (Canada), 1976.

Killinger, B. E. *Humour in psychotherapy—A shift to a new perspective*. Paper presented to the American Psychological Association Convention, Montreal, Canada, August 1980.

Koestler, A. *The act of creation*. New York: Macmillan, 1964.

Kohut, H. *The restoration of the self*. New York: International Universities Press, 1977.

Kris, E. Ego development and the comic. *International Journal of Psychoanalysis*, 1938, *19*, 77–90.

Kris, E. Laughter as an expressive process: Contributions to the psychoanalysis of expressive behavior. *International Journal of Psychoanalysis*, 1940, *21*, 314–341.

Kubie, L. S. The destructive potential of humor in psychotherapy. *American Journal of Psychiatry*, 1971, *127*, 861–866. Copyright 1971, the American Psychiatric Association.

Kuhlman, T. L. Symptom relief through insight during systematic desensitization: A case study. *Psychotherapy: Theory, Research, & Practice*, 1982, *19*, 88–94.

Lamb, C. S. The use of paradoxical intention: self-management through laughter. *Personnel and Guidance Journal*, 1980, *59*, 217–219.

Lambo, T. A. Schizophrenia and borderline states. In A. V. S. DeReuck & R. Porter (Eds.), *Transcultural psychiatry*. Boston: Little, Brown, 1965, 62–75.

Langevin, R., & Day, H. I. Physiological correlates of humor. In J. H. Goldstein & P. E. McGhee (Eds.), *The psychology of humor*. New York: Academic Press, 1972, 129–142.

LeBon, G. *The crowd: A study of the popular mind*. London: T. Fisher Unwin, 1896.

Lenrow, P. B. Use of metaphor in facilitating constructive behavior change. *Psychotherapy: Theory, Research, & Practice*, 1966, *3*, 145–148.

Levine, J. Humor as a form of therapy. In A. J. Chapman & H. C. Foot (Eds.), *It's a funny thing, humour*. Oxford, U.K.: Pergamon, 1977, 127–139.

Levine, J., & Redlich, F. C. Failure to understand humor. *Psychoanalytic Quarterly*, 1955, *24*, 560–572.

Loewald, E. The development and uses of humour in a four-year-old's treatment. *International Review of Psychoanalysis*, 1976, *3*, 209–221.

Loewenstein, R. M. Variations in classical technique: Concluding remarks. *International Journal of Psychoanalysis*, 1958, *39*, 240–242.

MacKinnon, R. A., & Michels, R. *The psychiatric interview in clinical practice*. Philadelphia: W. B. Saunders, 1971.

Malan, D. H. *The frontier of brief psychotherapy*. New York: Plenum Press, 1976.

Malone, T. P., Whitaker, C. A., Warkentin, J., & Felder, R. E. Rational and nonrational psychotherapy. *American Journal of Psychotherapy*, 1961, *15*, 212–220

Martineau, W. H. A model of the social functions of humor. In J. H. Goldstein & P. E. McGhee (Eds.), *The psychology of humor*. New York: Academic Press, 1972, 101–128.

McGhee, P. E. *Humor: Its origin and development*. San Francisco: W. H. Freeman, 1979.

Meichenbaum, D. *Cognitive-behavior modification: An integrative approach*. New York: Plenum Press, 1977.

Mendel, W. H. (Ed.). *A celebration of laughter*. Los Angeles: Mara Books, 1970.

Mindess, H. *Laughter and liberation*. Los Angeles: Nash, 1971.

Mindess, H. Hail to the chiefs. *American Psychologist*, 1975, *30*, 598–600.

Mindess, H. The use and abuse of humour in psychotherapy. In A. J. Chapman & H. C. Foot (Eds.), *Humour and laughter: Theory, research, and applications*. London: John Wiley & Sons, 1976, 331–341. Copyright 1976 by John Wiley & Sons, Ltd. Reprinted by permission.

Mindess, H. *On the limits of laughter*. Paper presented to the American Psychological Association Convention, Los Angeles, August 1981.

Minuchin, S., & Fishman, H. C. *Family therapy techniques*. Cambridge, Mass.: Harvard University Press, 1981.

Monro, D. H. *Argument of laughter*. Melbourne: University of Melbourne Press, 1951.

Nelson, M. C. Effects of paradigmatic techniques on the psychic economy of borderline patients. *Psychiatry*, 1962, *25*, 119–134. Copyright © 1962 by the William Alanson White Psychiatric Foundation, Inc.

Nerhardt, G. Humor and inclination to laugh: Emotional reactions to stimuli of different divergence from a range of expectancy. *Scandinavian Journal of Psychology*, 1970, *11*, 185–195.

Nussbaum, K., & Michaux, W. W. Response to humor in depression: A predictor and evaluator of patient change. *Psychiatric Quarterly*, 1963, *37*, 527–539.

O'Connell, W. E. The adaptive functions of wit and humor. *Journal of Abnormal & Social Psychology*, 1960, *61*, 263–270.

O'Connell, W. E. Frankl, Adler, and spirituality. *Journal of Religion and Health*, 1972, *11*, 134–138.

O'Connell, W. E. *Action therapy and Adlerian theory.* Chicago: Alfred Adler Institute, 1975.

O'Connell, W. E. The demystification of Sister Saint Nobody. *Journal of Individual Psychology*, 1979, *35*, 79–94.

O'Connell, W. E. The natural high therapist: God's favorite monkey. *Voices*, 1981, *16*, 37–44.(a)

O'Connell, W. E. Natural high therapy. In R. Corsini (Ed.), *Innovative psychotherapies.* New York: John Wiley & Sons, 1981, 554–568. (b)

Olson, H. A. The use of humor in psychotherapy. *Individual Psychologist*, 1976, *13*, 34–37.

Orfanidis, M. M. Children's use of humor in psychotherapy. *Social Casework*, 1972, *53*, 147–155. Published by Family Service Association of America.

Peter, L. J. *The laughter prescription.* New York: Ballantine Books, 1982.

Poland, W. S. The place of humor in psychotherapy. *American Journal of Psychiatry*, 1971, *128*, 127–129. Copyright 1971, the American Psychiatric Association.

Radcliffe-Brown, A. R. On joking relationships. *Africa*, 1940, *13*, 195–210.

Radcliffe-Brown, A. R. A further note on joking relationships. *Africa*, 1949, *19*, 133–140.

Reik, T. *The inner experience of a psychoanalyst.* London: George Allen & Unwin, 1949.

Rice, L. N. The evocative functions of the therapist. In D. A. Wexler & L. N. Rice (Eds.), *Innovations in client-centered therapy.* New York: John Wiley & Sons, 1974, 289–313.

Rimm, D. C., & Masters, J. C. *Behavior therapy: Techniques and empirical findings:* New York: Academic Press, 1974.

Roberts, A. F., & Johnson, D. M. Some factors related to the perception of funniness in humor stimuli. *Journal of Social Psychology*, 1957, *46*, 57–63.

Roncoli, M. Bantering: A therapeutic strategy with obsessional patients. *Perspective in Psychiatric Care*, 1974, *12*, 171–175.

Rose, G. J. King Lear and the use of humor in treatment. *Journal of the American Psychoanalytic Association*, 1969, *17*, 927–940.

Rosen, A., & Proctor, E. K. Distinctions between treatment outcomes and their implications for treatment evaluation. *Journal of Consulting & Clinical Psychology*, 1981, *49*, 418–425.

Rosen, V. H. Variants of comic caricatures and their relationship to obsessive-compulsive phenomena. *Journal of the American Psychoanalytic Association,* 1963, *11,* 704–724.

Rosenheim, E. Humor in psychotherapy: An interactive experience. *American Journal of Psychotherapy,* 1974, *28,* 584–591.

Rosenheim, E. Humor in psychotherapy. In J. Masserman (Ed.), *Current psychiatric therapies,* 1976, *16,* 59–65.

Rouff, L. L. Creativity and sense of humor. *Psychological Reports,* 1975, *37,* 1022.

Rule, W. R. Increasing self-modeled humor. *Rational Living,* 1977, *12,* 7–9.

Salzman, L. *The obsessive personality.* New York: Science House, 1968.

Schachter, S., & Wheeler, L. Epinephrine, chlorpromazine, and amusement. *Journal of Abnormal & Social Psychology,* 1962, *65,* 121–129.

Schimel, J. L. The function of wit and humor in psychoanalysis. *Journal of the American Academy of Psychoanalysis,* 1978, *6,* 369–379.

Schofield, W. *Psychotherapy: The purchase of friendship.* Englewood Cliffs, N.J.: Prentice-Hall, 1964.

Searles, H. F. The place of neutral therapist-responses in psychotherapy with the schizophrenic patient. *International Journal of Psychoanalysis,* 1963, *44,* 42–56.

Shaw, C. R. The use of humor in child psychiatry. *American Journal of Psychotherapy,* 1961, *15,* 368–381.

Shelton, J. L., & Ackerman, J. M. *Homework in counseling and psychotherapy.* Springfield, Ill.: Charles C Thomas, 1973.

Singer, J. L. *Imagery and daydream methods in psychotherapy and behavior modification.* New York: Academic Press, 1974.

Smith, R. E. The use of humor in the counterconditioning of anger responses: A case study. *Behavior Therapy,* 1973, *4,* 576–580. Copyright 1973 by the Association for the Advancement of Behavior Therapy. Reprinted by permission of the publisher and the author.

Sperling, S. J. On the psychodynamics of teasing. *Journal of the American Psychoanalytic Association,* 1953, *1,* 458–483.

Stearns, F. R. *Laughing.* Springfield, Ill.: Charles C Thomas, 1972.

Sullivan, H. S. *The psychiatric interview.* New York: W. W. Norton, 1949.

Sully, J. *Essay on laughter.* New York: Longmans-Green, 1902.

Tarachow, S. Interpretation and reality in psychotherapy. *International Journal of Psychoanalysis,* 1962, *43,* 377–387.

Tolor, A. Observations on joke-telling by children in therapy. *Mental Hygiene,* 1966, *50,* 295–296.

Van Den Aardweg, G. J. A grief theory of homosexuality. *American Journal of Psychotherapy,* 1974, *26,* 52–68.

Vargas, M. J. Uses of humor in group psychotherapy. *Group Psychotherapy,* 1961, *14,* 198–202.

Ventis, W. L. Case history: The use of laughter as an alternative response in systematic desensitization. *Behavior Therapy,* 1973, *4,* 120–122.

Ventis, W. L. Humor in behavior therapy. In H. Mindess & J. Turek (Eds.), *The Study of Humor.* Los Angeles: Antioch University, 1980, 16–23.

Verma, L. K. Humour differences among creative and non-creative high school students from various academic streams. *Indian Psychological Review,* 1981, *20,* 1–6.

Wachtel, P. L. *Psychoanalysis and behavior therapy.* New York: Basic Books, 1977.

Washburn, R. W. A study of smiling and laughter in infants in the first year of life. *Genetic Psychology Monographs,* 1929, *6,* 397–535.

Watzlawick, P. A review of double bind theory. *Family Process,* 1963, *2,* 132–153.

Watzlawick, P. *The language of change.* New York: Basic Books, 1978.

Watzlawick, P., Weakland, J., & Fisch, R. *Change: Principles of problem formation and problem resolution.* New York: W. W. Norton, 1974.

Weeks, G. R., & L'Abate, L. *Paradoxical psychotherapy.* New York: Brunner/ Mazel, 1982.

Weiner, I. B. *Principles of psychotherapy.* New York: John Wiley & Sons, 1975.

Whitaker, C. A., Felder, R. E. Malone, T. P., & Warkentin, J. First stage techniques in the experiential psychotherapy of chronic schizophrenic patients. In J. Masserman (Ed.), *Current psychiatric therapies,* 1962, *2,* 147–158.

Whitaker, C. A., & Malone, T. P. *The roots of psychotherapy.* London: Blakiston Publishers, 1953.

Wilkins, W. Desensitization: Social and cognitive factors underlying the effectiveness of Wolpe's procedures. *Psychological Bulletin,* 1971, *76,* 311–317.

Wilmer, H. A. *Social psychiatry in action.* Springfield, Ill.: Charles C Thomas, 1958.

Wilson, C. P. *Jokes: Form, content, use and function.* London: Academic Press, 1979.

Wolfenstein, M. *Children's humor.* Glencoe, Ill.: Free Press, 1954.

Yalom, I. D. *The theory and practice of group psychotherapy.* New York: Basic Books, 1970.

Yates, A. J. *Theory and practice in behavior therapy.* New York: John Wiley & Sons, 1975.

Yorukoglu, A. Children's favorite jokes and their relation to emotional conflicts. *Journal of the American Academy of Child Psychiatry,* 1974, *13,* 677–690.

Zillmann, D., et al. Acquisition of information from educational television programs as a function of differently paced humorous inserts. *Journal of Educational Psychology,* 1980, *72,* 170–180.

Ziv, A. The influence of humourous atmosphere on divergent thinking. *Contemporary Educational Psychology,* 1983, *8,* 68–75.

Zuk, G. H. A further study of laughter in family therapy. *Family Process,* 1964, *3,* 77–89.

Zuk, G. H. On the theory and pathology of laughter in psychotherapy. *Psychotherapy: Theory, Research, & Practice,* 1966, *3,* 97–101.

Zuk, G. H., Boszormenyi-Nagy, I., & Heiman, E. Some dynamics of laughter during family therapy. *Family Process*, 1963, *2*, 302–314.

Zwirling, I. The favorite joke in diagnostic and therapeutic interviewing. *Psychoanalytic Quarterly*, 1955, *24*, 104–114.

Author Index

Subject Index

Therapist as support system, 75
Tickling, 11
Transference, 30–31, 39, 87, 98

Visual imagery, 39, 47
We-group/we-ness, 104–6